Other books by Thom S. Rainer

Transformational Church (coauthor)
Simple Life (coauthor)
Vibrant Church (coauthor)
Essential Church (coauthor)
Raising Dad (coauthor)
Simple Church (coauthor)
The Challenge of the Great Commission (coeditor)
The Unexpected Journey
Breakout Churches
The Unchurched Next Door
Surprising Insights from the Unchurched
Eating the Elephant (revised edition) (coauthor)
High Expectations
The Every Church Guide to Growth (coauthor)
The Bridger Generation
Effective Evangelistic Churches
The Church Growth Encyclopedia (coeditor)
Experiencing Personal Revival (coauthor)
Giant Awakenings
Biblical Standards for Evangelists (coauthor)
Eating the Elephant
The Book of Church Growth
Evangelism in the Twenty-first Century

the millennials

Connecting to
America's
Largest Generation

THOM S. RAINER & JESS W. RAINER

B&H
PUBLISHING GROUP
Nashville, Tennessee

LifeWay
RESEARCH
Biblical Solutions for Life

978-1-4336-7003-9

Published by B&H Publishing Group
Nashville, Tennessee

Dewey Decimal Classification: 305.2
Subject Heading: SOCIAL GROUPS /
GENERATION Y—RESEARCH \
POPULATION—IDENTITY

1 2 3 4 5 6 7 8 • 14 13 12 11

From Thom

To the three Millennial couples who bring me great joy

Sam and Erin Rainer

Art and Sarah Rainer

Jess and Rachel Rainer

And always

To Nellie Jo

Our sons chose wives who are like you.

That means they chose the best.

From Jess

To Rachel

My beautiful wife and my best friend

Your support is unceasing.

Your love is unending.

You are a blessing from God.

I love you.

Contents

Acknowledgments

As a father/son team, we found a certain joy in writing this book. We are both adults, but we still enjoy each other's fellowship. We have busy lives with our own immediate families and work. But this book forced us to spend time together. It was an adventure we will never forget and never take for granted. We are two blessed men to have this opportunity.

It takes a large team to write a book, and we are grateful that we are on the team called LifeWay Christian Resources and B&H Publishing Group. Our deepest gratitude goes to Brad Waggoner, the publisher of B&H, and Tom Walters, our always competent and always encouraging editor. Of course, we also need to thank literally dozens more on the B&H team. Though their names are not printed here, we know that this book would not be a reality without them.

Stacy Edwards' official title is executive assistant to the president. But she always goes above and beyond on projects she attempts. We are both so grateful for the careful editing she did on this book and the research she prepared at the onset of this project. This book is so much better because of Stacy's usual outstanding work.

Our thanks also goes to LifeWay Research and its leaders, Ed Stetzer and Scott McConnell. These two men have provided outstanding leadership to what has become the premier Christian research organization in the world. The work they did on the Millennials is incredible. This book is mostly based on that research.

This book is based on the surveys of twelve hundred Millennials representing most subgroups in the United States. We are so grateful for their responses. Both of us spoke to other Millennials beyond these twelve hundred, but that original group represents the core of the research. Some of the comments made in this book are composite stories of several Millennials. All of the comments represent the facts of the research and the perspectives they told us.

Most of this book is written for those of varying perspectives, including religious perspectives. We are aware, however, that no book is written without some bias. Undoubtedly our bias as evangelical Christians will show at times. Still, we tried to maintain objectivity throughout the book.

We are also indebted to Dr. Natalie Clark Winter of California Baptist University. Dr. Winter serves as associate dean of the Dr. Robert K. Jabs School of Business and associate professor of Marketing. Her seminal work on Millennials and consultation with us proved invaluable in helping us shape the research and this book. Dr. Winter can be reached at www.ConcurrentCommunications.com.

● ● ● ●

From Thom

I have a reputation of being overboard crazy about my family. I will admit to a certain level of insanity about my wife, my sons, my daughters-in-law, and my grandchildren. I guess you could say I am crazy in love with all of them.

Everyone who knows Nellie Jo loves her. I just happen to be the guy who got to marry her thirty-three years ago. She is my biggest fan on every project I do, including being crazy enough to write or coauthor twenty-three books. I love that girl. She is the love of my life, and she is my best friend.

My three sons bring me unspeakable joy. Every time I get a call, text, e-mail, tweet, or Skype from one of the boys, my day is brighter. Of course, anyone who knows me knows how much I love Sam, Art, and Jess. I have been talking about them incessantly since the days they were born. All three boys had the incredible wisdom to marry superior wives, just as I did. I had no idea how much I could love daughters-in-law, but I do. Their names are Erin, Sarah, and Rachel, and they are the closest things to daughters I have ever known.

I can't imagine any greater honor and joy than working on a book with my son. Jess is an incredible writer, a creative thinker, and an untiring worker. The book has both of our names on it, but he deserves most of the credit. Though we experienced the weariness that is common with authors who have deadlines,

I am really sad that the book is done. The time with my youngest son has been time that I will treasure forever.

I must mention my three grandchildren: Canon, Maggie, and Nathaniel. What incredible joys all three of them are to Nellie Jo and me! They keep us young and keep us joyous.

So why do I mention my family at the beginning of a book? It's simple. I would be nothing, and I could do nothing without their love, support, and encouragement. I am a man who is so incredibly blessed.

●   ●   ●   ●

From Jess

It is hard for me even to begin to write how blessed I feel for all those who are a part of this book. The time spent writing this book was filled with support from neighbors, coworkers, professors, pastors, friends, and family. Many people played many different roles in allowing me to find the time and energy to write.

My family is the biggest source of encouragement and support that I can possibly imagine. Even though my in-laws are hundreds of miles away, their joy in seeing this book come to life was felt every step of the way. Bryan, Sarah, and Emma, thank you for your encouragement. John and Linda, thank you for your prayers. Most importantly, thanks for raising a godly daughter.

Sam and Art, my two big brothers, thanks for paving the way for me as an author. More importantly, thanks for paving the way for me in life. Your leadership is valued and emulated. I have always followed you both. And I will continue to follow.

Mom, you deserve more recognition than the number of pages in this book. I will never stop singing your praises. Your unconditional love and dedication to your three sons is unmatched. I appreciate your great sacrifices. Thank you for the love, care, and nurture you unselfishly give. Thank you for showing me Jesus. Your heavenly reward will be great.

Dad, I would never be able to write these words without you. Your passion for your three sons is tremendous. Your sense of pride for me makes me feel as if I can accomplish anything. Thank you for being my friend, mentor, and loving father. Your godly leadership is without comparison. I pray that I can be half the father to my children that you are to me.

Canon, you make me the most proud father. The moment your mother and I met you for the first time produced nothing but pure joy. Although you are just past your first birthday, you are already such a smart, talented, handsome young man. You will be such a wonderful big brother. I am so excited to see what the Lord has planned for your life. And no matter what happens in your life, I will always be proud of you. I love you.

Rachel, you are a constant source of encouragement and support. I never would have been able to take on a project of this nature without you. Your strength carried me through the months of writing this book. Thank you for your sacrifice.

Thank you for taking extra care of our son, Canon. Thank you for the love you give me. I am truly undeserving of you. You are a woman of God who will continue to be used in mighty ways. I love you so much.

CHAPTER 1

Meet the Millennials

D on't stereotype me or my generation."

Her name is Emily. Our team was supposed to be interviewing her, but she had a knack for making us the respondents. This time she was suggesting how we approach our research project. Perhaps "suggesting" is not the best way to say it. She was telling us what to do.

But Emily was right. You cannot really stereotype her or anyone in her generation. In many ways this generation is the most diverse generation in America's history. More on that later.

So why spend thousands of hours researching and writing about a generation that, in some ways, defies description? In the case of Emily's generation, we readily admit that any attempt to describe their behavioral and cognitive patterns will never satisfactorily represent any one segment of the larger group. But we do believe it is helpful to understand this generation with all of its diversity and to touch on some common themes that have touched a large number of its group.

By the way, we are talking about the Millennial Generation, a group of young people whose birth years range from 1980 to 2000. This generation edged out the Boomers (aka the Baby Boomers born 1946 to 1964) to become the largest generation in America's history.

We'll talk more about the demographics of this generation later in this chapter. For now we see the sheer size of this generation, and it takes our breath away. Nearly seventy-eight million live births took place between 1980 and 2000. The Millennials are already impacting businesses, the workplace, schools, churches, and many more organizations. Frankly, if we don't learn more about this generation, we are doing them and ourselves a disservice. They are just too big to ignore.

For those of us who've been around awhile, we are familiar with all the fuss about the Boomers. That generation garnered incredible attention because of its sheer size. Companies wanted their business. Politicians wanted their votes. Schools wanted their enrollment. Churches wanted their attendance. And charities wanted their contributions.

Now a new generation has emerged, and they are slightly larger than the Boomers. We saw the impact these young people could have in the 2008 presidential election. The eighteen- to twenty-nine-year-old Millennials voted for Barack Obama by an overwhelming sixty-six to thirty-two margin. This generation spoke, and they got their president.

And the impact they are making is just beginning.

Emily is right. She was born in 1987, and she is part of a diverse generation. Still, that diversity does not mean we can't learn key facets about her age cohorts. Some things are already changing with the Millennials.

For example, the Millennials are on track to become America's most educated generation. In 2007, the first year the twenty-five- to twenty-nine-year-old age group was entirely comprised of Millennials, 30 percent had attained a college degree. That is the highest rate ever recorded for that age group.

As another example, Millennials are marrying much later, if at all. In 1970 about 44 percent of eighteen- to twenty-five-year-old Boomers were married. Today only 15 percent of Millennials in that age group are married. And the average age of first marriages has gone up from 20.8 for women in 1970 to 25.5 today. For men the average age of first marriages has increased from 23.2 to 27.5 over that same period.

One more significant change is worth noting from the Boomer generation to the Millennials. About 65 percent of young adults cohabit at least once prior to marriage, compared to just 10 percent in the 1960s.

But we are getting ahead of ourselves. We have much to unpack about the Millennial Generation in the chapters to come. For now let's take a look at our study and how we got the information for this book.

The Millennial Study

Our study was a researcher's dream in many ways. We had the incredible opportunity to hear from twelve hundred Millennials across the country. Our representative sample included American adults born between 1980 and 1991. So to be clear, our study is on the older Millennials. We did not include those born between 1992 and 2000.

How accurate is our study? At a 95 percent confidence level and a 50 percent response distribution, the potential sampling error on this national study is +/- 2.8 percentage points. Okay, we admit it. The previous statement is not very exciting unless you are a statistical nerd. Simply stated, this research is pretty accurate. You can trust the statistical validity of our work.

We tried hard to keep this study bias free at the design stage of the research instrument, to the actual survey process, and to the interpretation of the data and writing of this book. Still we realize that biases may have crept in at some points, so we want you to know just a bit about our backgrounds.

We are both evangelical Christians. Though we are unapologetic about our faith, we have tried to be objective as we asked and interpreted the questions. We realized early in this process that our beliefs represented a minority of the Millennials, and we wanted to be fair in our assessments and conclusions.

Millennials represent a more diverse group than do any previous American generations. Respondents in this study were a demographically representative sample of U.S. Millennials in all of their diversity. Whites are still a majority at 61 percent, but that number is lower than previous generations. African-Americans accounted for 14 percent of our sample, Hispanics, 19 percent; Asians, 5 percent; and mixed, 1 percent.

Gender representation was very balanced. Males accounted for 51 percent of the respondents, and females accounted for 49 percent. The percentage of respondents from each birth year, 1980 to 1991, ranged from 8 percent to 10 percent, with the exception of the birth years 1990 and 1991, where the percentage was 7 percent and 4 percent respectively. Again our point is to demonstrate the balance and valid representation of the sample.

Matters such as education, income, and geographical distribution reflect similar distribution of the entire generation. We could belabor all these points and bore you to death. We do want you to have confidence in our study.

Respondents were asked a series of questions with most of them requiring an objective response. Some of the questions, however, were open-ended, and the Millennial was able to go any direction he or she desired. That part of the study, though difficult to capture in percentages and trends, included some of the most fascinating and fun work of this project. You will hear many of the comments of the Millennials throughout this book. Most of them were not shy!

Our research team began the process by deciding what we wanted to hear from the Millennials. Some of the questions represent the perspectives of the old man (Thom), while others reflect the younger view of the Millennial coauthor (Jess). Others had input as well.

Some of the categories where we asked questions include:

- What's really important in your life? What truly matters?
- What is your attitude about the environment? Are you really as green as the anecdotal information suggests?
- What are your attitudes about money and other financial matters? Do you have plans for you own finances?
- What types of work environment do you like or not like? How do you choose a job?
- Are you optimistic or pessimistic about the future? How will you impact the future world in which you will live?
- To whom do you turn for guidance? Are you more likely to be a loner or to seek help?
- What are your views on leadership? How do you view leaders today?
- What are your attitudes about marriage? How important is family to you?
- How important are other relationships such as friends and coworkers?
- What technology tools do you like and use? How involved are you in social media?
- What are your spiritual views? How often are you involved in spiritual activities?

The journey to learn more about this generation was fascinating. At many points in the study, we were greatly encouraged. The Millennials are a generation that has hope for the future. Indeed, they are a generation that, as a whole, wants to make a positive difference for the future. Nearly nine out of ten respondents indicated that they feel responsible to make a difference in this world.

They are the Millennial Generation, the largest generation in America's history. Before we delve more fully into the facts, hopes, dreams, and attitudes of this generation, let's take a brief excursion into the previous generations. The Millennials are, as the name states, the generation to take us into a new century and a new millennium. The previous century, however, was populated largely by four other generations: the G.I. Generation; the Silent Generation; the Boomers; and Generation X.

The Generations Before

Emily shared with us some of her dreams and aspirations. "I really plan to make some contribution to this world in my lifetime. I don't care if I rise to the top of an organization or become a political power broker," she said. "I just want to make a contribution."

This attitude is pervasive among the Millennials. The young men and women we surveyed are, as a rule, not focusing as much on self as they are on how they can make a difference. This one insight has enormous implications. They are the largest generation in America's history, and they want to make a contribution. Compare this attitude with that of the Boomers, a huge generation only slightly smaller than the Millennials. The Boomers have been largely self-absorbed and narcissistic. Imagine the change our nation could experience if the dominant attitude in America shifts from entitled to giving.

But let's back up even farther than the Boomer Generation and get a glimpse of all the generations that shaped our nation. First, look at the relative population size of each of the generations:

G.I. Generation (1904–1924)	59.6 million (live births)
Silent Generation (1925–1945)	55.4 million
Boomer Generation (1946–1964)	75.9 million
Gen X (1965–1979)	51.5 million
Millennial Generation (1980–2000)	77.9 million

As we will note later, generations can be defined in a number of ways. Although we don't reject other definitions, our primary determination of a generation was demographic. We simply looked at the pattern of live births, with no one generation exceeding twenty-one years in length.

Let's take the much-discussed Boomer Generation as an example. The number of live births spiked significantly from 1945 to 1946 reaching over three million (3.4 million) for the first time in our nation's history. Thus the "boom" began in 1946. Live births peaked above four million from 1954 to 1964, but then dropped dramatically in 1965 to 3.7 million. Thus the boom ended and a new generation, Gen X, began.

With that definition in mind, let's look at the five generations of the twentieth century. Of course, we recognize that the

Millennials take us into the twenty-first century and into a new millennium.

G.I. Generation. The fairly stable population of this generation was most affected by two events: the Great Depression and World War II. The latter event gave the generation their name.

The members of this generation are some of the most powerful people our nation has known. They are the first full generation to enjoy the benefits of Social Security, yet their affluence was set even without Social Security.

This generation includes nearly sixty million men and women, though the majority of them are no longer living. For most of their lives, the G.I. Generation benefited from an expanding economy, rising real estate values, and generous government programs. Interestingly, their wealth has not depended on lengthy education. A high school education was sufficient to find a good-paying, secure job with good benefits in their early years. Because they typically had a lower level of education than successor generations, their perspectives on life tended to be shaped differently from the younger population.

Silent Generation. The generation born from 1925 to 1945 got a bad deal with its name. They were called the Silent Generation because few of its members held high-profile business or political positions at the time of its naming. For example, no United States president has come from this generation. However, not as many demographers call them the Silent Generation today. They eventually became leaders of major corporations, and many came into powerful positions of governmental and political leadership. Some decided to call this generation the Swing Generation because they were caught between two potent and influential generations: the G.I. Generation and the Boomer Generation. Some of the generation swing toward the more casual lifestyle commonplace with the Boomers; others swing to the more conservative perspectives of their G.I. Generation elders.

Not only did this generation ultimately have influence; they also had considerable affluence. Competition for first entry-level, then middle-management, and then upper-management positions was not as intense for the G.I. Generation. The supply of positions available was high for the number in the generation. Some demographers have even suggested that, with the present economic scenario, this group may be the last generation to enjoy affluence in their retirement years.

Boomer Generation. They have been commonly called the Baby Boomers, those born between 1946 and 1964. Until the Millennials, this generation was the largest in America's history. In many ways the Boomers are the most discussed, most marketed, and most debated generation ever. Their sheer size caught the attention of businesses, schools, the media, churches, and other organizations for decades. Whatever this generation did, many would follow. They are the generation that brought us bell-bottom pants and minivans. They pressed the nation for housing and jobs. Now the United States will have to cope with the Boomers' demands for Social Security benefits.

The majority of the Boomers were raised by stay-at-home mothers who were younger than mothers with children at home today. They are the Woodstock and the Vietnam generation that believed their way was *the* way. In the 1960s the Boomers were countercultural and antiauthoritarian. That self-centered, independent spirit became a self-centered, materialistic spirit in the 1980s. By the decade of the nineties, the importance of the Boomers became apparent in the growth of New Age spiritualism and the self-help movement.

By 1995 three out of ten living Americans were Boomers. No generation had its own generational literary genre until the Boomers. Hundreds of books have been written on the generation, and the writing continues today.

Gen X. They were originally called the Buster Generation because of the dramatic decline in live births from their predecessor generation. In 1965, the first year of the baby bust, live births dropped below 3.8 million. The number of births had been over four million since 1954. The trend continued until 1980 when live births once again began a significant upturn.

Generation X or, more commonly Gen X, is the label that stuck. This name came from a nondescript novel by Douglas Coupland. Though most of the generation members really don't like any of the names, Gen X is the label of choice for the rest of the population.

Gen X members are sometimes called slackers, supposedly because of their poor work ethic. But the critics are typically condescending Boomers who really don't have their facts straight. This generation is no less diligent than any previous generation, especially the Boomers. Those in this generation are also sometimes stereotyped as pessimists, perhaps with reason. From an economic viewpoint Gen X entered the job market during difficult times. It is hardly surprising that they are both cautious and pessimistic about their long-term financial prospects.

And Now the Millennials

If Americans had an unusual fascination with the large Boomer population, it will be matched, if not exceeded, with their focus on the Millennials. Because of the comparable size of the two generations, the parallels between the two population groups are already remarkable.

As the Boomers shaped so much of the American culture for most of the last half of the twentieth century, so the Millennials will for the first half of the twenty-first century. They will be the dominant adult population during that period, and thus many organizations will seek to win their favor. Indeed, some organizations are already getting that message today and responding accordingly. The Millennials will be moving into positions of power and influence as this new millennium progresses.

It will be fascinating to see how individuals and organizations will respond. We will likely see the same preoccupation with this generation as with the Boomer Generation. It thus behooves us to learn as much about the Millennials as we can at this stage. Such is the purpose of this book.

Understanding the Millennial Years

Some have a misperception that generational studies are clearly defined. Everyone agrees, some surmise, on the generational names and generational years. Such is simply not the case. The matter of the generational span seems to have the most variations. What determines the birth-year range of the Millennials, Gen X, Boomers, and others?

We have found that the variation of claims for generational span tends to fall into one of two categories. The first is the number of live births per year, a simple demographic pattern. For example, in 1946 the number of live births spiked dramatically and continued to 1964. Thus our nation experienced a baby boom, and the Boomer Generation took hold. The second category for defining generational years is grouping people according to common historical experiences and behavior.

The reality is that most generational studies use both categories, though they may emphasize one factor over another. Since we are both somewhat statistical nerds (Okay, Thom admits it, and Jess isn't so sure), we tend to lean more toward a pure demographic definition for the Millennial Generation. In other words, we are more likely to look for some pattern in the number of live births by year.

In the case of the Millennials, there was a clear spike in the number of live births in 1980. In fact the number of live births per year had been well below 3.5 million since 1972 until the spike occurred. Then in 1980 live births soared not only above 3.5 million but also above 3.6 million. A new boom had begun.

This second baby boom continued to grow and stabilized around four million live births per year from 1989 to 2000. The baby boom was not really over in 2000, but most demographers do not take a generation beyond twenty to twenty-one years. Beyond that time the possibility of common experiences and behavior tend to diminish.

Forgive us if this excursion caused you to yawn. We simply wanted to be clear on why we chose 1980 to 2000 as the generational years for the Millennials. Others do have some variation from us, but we are all fairly close in our assumptions.

What's in a Generational Name?

Typically a generational name goes through several variations before one tends to stick. That was certainly true with the Millennials. In fact Thom attempted to be one of the first to name this generation with his book *The Bridger Generation*. The term *bridger* means that this generation will be a bridge from one millennium to the next. In fact, Thom even attempted to name the four successive generations alliteratively: Builders, Boomers, Busters, and Bridgers. Jess found it humorous that Thom was not successful in any of these endeavors.

But Thom was not the only one whose generational name did not stick. There have been a number of other attempts. Several failed names fall into the category of connection with another generation. Generation Y and Generation XX attempted to connect the Millennials with Gen X. And Echo

Boom and Boomer Babies obviously attempted a connection to the Boomer generation.

It would seem that these naming attempts were unsuccessful because many of the Millennials want their generation's name to stand on its own. "We are not an extension of another generation," Archie told us. "We are really different from either Gen X or the Boomers. Don't try to stick us with a name that reflects our dependence on either one of those messed-up groups."

Archie obviously was not thrilled with his two predecessor generations.

Generation Tech did not stick either. Shonda, born in 1986, speaks to that name. "Good grief. We don't want to be identified with just technology. See how the Boomers would react if you called them Generation Television."

Good point.

Still other attempts failed. Generation Next was one. "What a stupid name," Hank exclaimed. "You could name every new generation with that name." Yet other unsuccessful labels include Generation 2000 and Generation.com.

The Millennials as a name for this generation stuck. Why and how did this name rise to the top? Our honest response is that we don't know. We do have our theories though. The Millennials themselves seem to like this name. At least they are not negative about it.

Probably the best explanation is related to an understanding of the millennial event. As its name indicates, a new millennium happens only once in a thousand years. The turning of this calendar day was monumental across the world. (Remember Y2K?) And only one generation can usher in this historic moment. Thus the new millennium is first in the hands, heads, and hearts of the Millennial. This is the name that thus gained momentum until it became a part of the everyday language of describing this generation.

They are the Millennials.

This book will delve into many facets of America's largest generation. For now let's look at some major themes we will encounter with the Millennials.

1 They Are Hopeful

One of the most amazing responses in our study was to a simple statement: "I believe I can do something great." First, the number of respondents who agreed is amazing. About 60 percent agreed strongly, and another 36 percent agreed somewhat. Of course, that's almost every respondent, 96 percent in total!

But the data based response needs unpacking. As much as the number is incredible in its sheer magnitude, the voices behind the numbers were even more telling. This is where the subjective responses in our study were extremely helpful. Millennials do not, as a generation, define greatness in the same way others may perceive it. When Thom was growing up as a Boomer in Alabama, he and his peers defined greatness in terms of fame, wealth, and personal power.

But Jess did not have that same perspective as a Millennial growing up in Louisville, Kentucky. He had great hope for greatness as did his Boomer predecessors, but the hope was not locked into the achievement of great wealth, fame, or power alone. Instead, if a Millennial does achieve wealth, fame, or power, it is a means to a greater good than an end in and of itself.

Sharon reflects this sentiment well. She was born in 1984 and has experienced early success as a registered nurse. She is continuing her education toward a doctorate so she can train other nurses in a university. "I have a good income," she began, "and that is not unimportant to me. I want to be financially successful. At least I want to be financially stable. I certainly have seen what can happen when you're not financially prepared for personal or economic crises. I mean, look how many people got wiped out in the Great Recession."

She continued her point. "But my desire for a good income is so I don't get sidetracked on my greater goals. I became a nurse because I really like helping people. It's good money, but there are better paying jobs out there. I then decided to pursue my doctorate because I saw that the nursing shortage might become a big issue as the Boomers become senior adults. I want to be able to be part of the training of the upcoming generation of nurses. That's how I want to make a difference."

Sharon also mentioned that nursing as a profession has a great opportunity to be on the scene when global tragedies strike. "When the Haiti earthquakes happened in early 2010, I was prepared to go," she explained. "I took two weeks vacation, and my employer was gracious enough to give me one extra week of paid leave. Those three weeks in Haiti were life changing for me. That's what I mean when I say I want to be great. I want to do something that makes a difference. I am doing something that makes a difference."

Sharon's attitude is pervasive among the Millennials. A significant majority of this generation was raised to be hopeful. Their dramatic birth-rate reversal was more than just a demographic measurement. The Gen X child era meant a huge emphasis on birth control, sometimes by abortion. But the Millennial parents ushered in a boom for fertility clinics. Millennials were given a clear message: children are valued. That message of hope is one staying with them through adulthood. Indeed the Millennials will become the greatest adopting generation our nation has known. Children are valued. Hope is instilled in them.

Thus we have a generation of optimists unlike the Gen X members before them. The Millennials tend to be upbeat, positive, and happy. But they are realists as well. They know that not all is well with the world. The Boomer Generation knew that and protested it. The Gen X Generation knew that and was depressed about it. And the Millennials know that, but they believe they can have a role in changing it.

If the G.I. Generation is truly the greatest generation, then the Millennials may be the greatest generation, part two. We are optimistic about the Millennials because they are hopeful about themselves.

#2

They Are Relational

Thom and Jess communicate with each other two to three times a week even though they live more than five hundred miles apart. By phone, e-mail, text, tweet, or Skype, they stay in touch. And there is one basic reason they do: they want to.

Thom is totally amazed that Jess and his two brothers want to stay in touch with their parents. After Thom reached adulthood, he called his parents once every other week, and they would reciprocate. In other words, one of them called once a week. It was planned, obligatory, and brief.

Now Thom wants to be clear that he loved his parents and they loved him (both are now deceased). But the connection between parent and child was not nearly as strong as it is between Thom and his sons. They stay in touch not because they have to but because they want to.

The Rainer family is not an aberration among the Millennials. Nearly nine out of ten (88 percent) told us that their parents had a positive influence on them. The family relationships are strong.

But the Millennials are relational beyond their immediate families. They have not let the avalanche of technological tools cause them to withdraw from personal contact with others. To the contrary, this generation seeks healthy relationships at work and beyond. "Connecting with people," Mandy told us, "is important to me. I'm on Facebook a lot, but I prefer to be with people. I love it when I meet a Facebook friend for the first time in person. It's like we have this instant connection."

We will delve into this issue in more detail in the book. But for now we can assert with confidence that the Millennial Generation is the relational generation.

#3 They Are Learners

Earlier we mentioned that Millennials are on the path to becoming the most educated generation in America's history. Already their rate of receiving undergraduate degrees has surpassed all previous generations. When we asked the respondents open-ended questions about what's really important in their lives, they listed education as the third most important, only behind family and friends.

This is the generation that scored higher on many of the aptitude tests in the 1990s. These young people are taking advanced placement tests in large numbers. They see education as cool and a college degree as a requisite to advance in life.

Why did the Millennials become the generation of learners? What makes them pursue education at such a frenetic pace? The answer seems to be twofold.

First, this generation isn't called the "helicopter generation" for no reason. Many of the Millennial parents hover over their children, especially in matters related to education. They lobby teachers for higher grades for their children and help their children in the application process for the best colleges. In his seminal work on the Millennials entering the workforce, *The Trophy Kids Grow Up*, Ronald Alsop notes that the parents of this generation are intensely involved with their kids from the cradle to the workplace.[1] Millennial parents have instilled in their children the vital importance of education to compete in the twenty-first century workforce.

Many Millennials thus really don't know another world other than one where they pursue education without question. And though many Millennial parents are overbearing, their efforts do have results. It is a competitive world, and education is often the differentiating point between a good job and a bad job, or landing a job and not landing a job. That brings us to the second reason this generation values learning and education.

Most Millennials are smart. They can read the realities of the marketplace. They know the trends in vocational opportunities. This pragmatic side increases the desire to learn, to get ahead, to get more education.

"I can see the trends," said Amy, born in 1987 in Sacramento. "I've heard some of the numbers about how much more a college graduate earns in a lifetime. And I recently read an article that said the unemployment rate for high school only graduates is twice as high as college graduates. It's really stupid not to invest a few more years in education. The payoff is huge."

#4

They Are Looking Less to Religion

This is the area that concerns both of us. We stated earlier in the chapter that we are evangelical Christians. And though we have attempted to offer objectivity in the process of this research, we admit that our biases will show from time to time. We'll try to bring your attention to it when they do.

The first alarm for us was sounded when we saw the responses to the importance of religion and spirituality to the Millennials. Keep in mind, we are not talking about Christianity or, more specifically, orthodox Christianity. We just offered them the question about any kind of religion or spirituality. The shocking reality for us is that only 13 percent of the Millennials considered any type of spirituality to be important in their lives.

We feared that this generation might be anti-Christian. In some ways the responses were worse than our fears. At least someone who opposes Christianity has our beliefs on his or her radar. Most of the Millennials don't think about religious matters at all.

Nathan is one of the older Millennials in our study. He was born in 1981. It's hard to pinpoint a home for him since his military family moved a lot. His last home was Texas. Unfortunately Nathan's responses were similar to many of the Millennials we interviewed.

"I really don't think that much about religion," he mused. "But I can see the pattern in my family. My grandparents attended a Southern Baptist church most of their lives. The little bit I know about religion or the Bible I got from them. But my parents only went to church on special occasions like Easter or Christmas Eve. And they sure didn't put any pressure on me to attend church. I really haven't thought about religion much in my life."

The picture became bleaker when the Millennials were asked about core values and doctrines of the Christian faith. For example, one of the cardinal doctrines of Christianity is the belief in the exclusivity of salvation in Jesus Christ. Stated simply, there is no way to heaven other than explicit faith in Christ.

This doctrine is at the heart of Christianity and is articulated at several points in the Bible. One example is John 14:6: "Jesus told him, 'I am the way, the truth, and the life. No one comes to the Father except through Me.'"

So how do Millennials respond when we ask them if Jesus is the only way to get to heaven? Only 31 percent strongly agree with this belief. The rest have a tepid belief in the doctrine, or they disagree with it altogether.

Perhaps Millennials are just too young to be focusing on matters of eternity. More than one-third of our respondents indicated that you couldn't really know what happens to you when you die. This generation is not just agnostic to God as revealed in Jesus Christ. They are agnostic toward all matters religious.

There are opportunities for Christians to be encouraged though. We will look at those reasons for encouragement later.

Meet the Millennials

We are optimistic and hopeful about this generation. We are not blind to some of the negative realities of the Millennials though. Millions of young people take drugs, have careless sex habits, and are affected by the worst of the pop culture. Many Millennials live in poverty, have absentee parents, and face a life of little hope. Thousands commit crimes and thousands are victims of crimes. We understand that, in any generation, horrific stories can be found and told.

But we are not looking at all the variant pieces of a generation as much as we are examining its center of gravity and its trends. From this high-level perch we can view a generation with optimism.

"My dad and I had a long talk today," Melanie told us. Melanie was twenty-five years old at the time of our interview. "We've had many good talks, but I really like this one. Dad really opened up about his generation and how it was when he was growing up. He told me about a bunch of pressures he faced and even admitted that he messed up on some occasions. He then began to tell me where many of his Boomer friends are today. There are really messed-up people in his generation. I know my generation is not perfect, but I think we've got it together better than previous generations. I really think we will make a big difference in this world."

So do we, Melanie. So do we.

This is the generation of Chelsea Clinton, Macaulay Culkin, and Christina Aguliera. It is also the generation of Britney Spears, Serena Williams, and Anna Kournikova. The Millennials include LeAnn Rimes, LeBron James, and Kirsten Dunst. This is the generation of Mary Kate Olsen and Ashley Olsen. It is also the generation of JonBenet Ramsey, a Millennial whose life ended much too soon.

But the years 1980 to 2000 include the births of millions of not-so-famous Millennials. They are ultimately the people who will shape and influence our culture for decades to come. One of those not-so-famous (at least not yet) people is the coauthor of this book, Jess Rainer. When Thom began thinking about doing a fresh and comprehensive study about this generation, he knew that he needed a younger mind, a representative of the Millennials, for the research and for the book to have true credibility.

So we are going to take a brief excursion in the next chapter and listen to the perspective of one Millennial who has both a love and a fascination for his peers. Research is indeed the gathering of data, but it is more than that. Good research involves good interpretation of the data. It's not just presenting a series of numbers. It is offering perspectives on what those numbers really mean.

That's where the perspective of a Millennial has been invaluable in this process. Let's now get ready to hear what all this research means to one of the generation.

His name is Jess. We now turn to his story.

1. Ronald Alsop, *The Trophy Kids Grow Up* (San Francisco: Jossey Bass, 2008); see especially chapter 3, "Apron Strings."

CHAPTER 2

A Millennial's Perspective

I am a people watcher.

I (Jess) must be careful in my admission though. Some may assume I am a person who habitually stares, but I assure you it is nothing of that nature. I simply take notice of the people and events that are taking place around me. Many people probably fall into this category. A people watcher tries to put all of his or her surroundings into perspective.

Take today for example. I notice in front of me are two young males talking. They both have laptops open, only their heads visible to each other. One of the young men holds his cell phone as if he is expecting an important call or text at any moment. Their conversation consists of abbreviated dialogue with long pauses between each statement.

Directly to their left are two young women listening intently to a story narrated by a third young woman. The narrator receives a text message, and the story stops abruptly. At the same time the other two young women check their cell phones to see if anything requires their attention. Once the young woman finishes replying to the text message, the story continues.

Three men sit at the table to my left. I only notice one BlackBerry between the three of them. The conversation appears too deep to be interrupted by an outside source at this point.

I take a moment to see who else surrounds me. I take a casual glance behind me. I find another young man typing on his laptop with earbuds in his ears. My guess is that he is listening to either iTunes or Pandora. He gives me a polite nod instead of saying hello.

And that leaves me. My laptop is open, iTunes playing, while I monitor my smart phone. I just turned off Skype but left Facebook open, just in case a notification pops up.

Every time I come to my local coffee shop, it is filled with similar scenes. The typical crowd is young, technologically savvy, and casually dressed. Each one of us is connected to a network through cell phones, laptops, and social media. Although there are subtle differences among us, there remains a common factor: we are all Millennials.

The previous chapter provided you a profile of the Millennials. We were born between 1980 and 2000 and are changing the American demographic. While the gender divide remains relatively equal, we have more minorities than previous genera-tions. Minorities make up 40 percent of the Millennials. Since I am giving my perspective of my generation, it is important to understand how I fit into the Millennial profile. It will provide the lens through which I view my generation.

Not the Typical Millennial

I am a white male born in April 1985. I have two older Millennial brothers, one who was born in 1982 and the other in 1980. My parents are still happily married with no previous marriages for either. My upbringing was immersed in evan-gelical Christian culture. I am the son of a pastor and attended Christian school from kindergarten through high school.

You might conclude that I'm not a typical Millennial, and you would be right. But our research found no stereotype for our generation. We are all different.

After high school I attended a secular state university where I graduated with a bachelor of science in finance. While in col-lege I met my beautiful wife, Rachel, and we married shortly after my graduation in June 2007. She also grew up in an evan-gelical Christian home but attended public schools through the duration of her education. Rachel is also a Millennial, born in December 1982.

Following our wedding, we moved to North Carolina so I could begin graduate school. I have been a retail banker since our arrival in North Carolina in 2007. The most recent life-changing event was the birth of our son, Canon John Rainer, in October 2009.

The Typical Millennial

I mentioned that I am not a typical Millennial. Even with a generation so diverse, some traits are more common than others. So what is the typical Millennial? The typical Millennial is not religious. The research shows that only one out of twenty hold the same religious beliefs as I do.

The typical Millennial is educated. Four out of five older Millennials received education beyond high school. One out of four graduated from college. Currently, one of four Millennials is in college.

The typical Millennial is working. With 50 percent of Millennials currently working, they are making a presence in the workforce.

The typical Millennial is not married, but keep in mind, the Millennials we studied were from eighteen to twenty-nine years old. They still have many years to tie the knot. For now, only one-fourth of these older Millennials are married. While most Millennials are not married now, most do plan to have children. Only about one out of ten said they planned to have no children.

Insights on the Millennials

In addition to understanding the typical Millennial, you also now have an understanding of who I am as a Millennial.

Through the massive amounts of research and data, I gathered ten insights into the Millennial Generation from the perspective of "one of them." Although mostly developed by the research, my insights also come from peer observation.

Through this research and observation I have discovered some of the defining elements of America's largest generation. It includes what we believe, what we think, and how we act. We truly are unlike any other generation. Let's see how we compare.

We want a connected family. This phrase almost seems oxymoronic. The definition of the family seems to change constantly. Over the past few decades it seems that the only constant with the family is that it is becoming more complex and disconnected. Divorce rates remain high; multiple marriages are commonplace; and domestic partnerships are increasing.

Many of today's families are complicated and, sadly, disconnected. This generation, however, offers hope. Millennials desire close relationships, and they just may be the ones to bring the family back together. While the return to a family of Mr. and Mrs. Jones with two children and a white picket fence is not likely, a Millennial's family will display a sense of connection unlike previous generations.

Millennials have traditional attitudes about the family. More than 80 percent of Millennials believe they will marry only once. Mark's perspective represents much of what his fellow Millennials view about family as well.

Mark is in his senior year of college. Since arriving at college, he feels that his family life has become more positive.

"It was hard spending every other weekend at my dad's [home]. Sometimes I wanted to be there longer, but sometimes I missed hanging out with my friends on the weekend."

His dad remarried during his freshman year of college. "I think he waited until I was no longer living with my mom. He didn't want to complicate things more than they already were."

Mark elaborated more about his feelings when he found out that his new stepmom was pregnant. "I think it surprised us all, especially my dad. It's cool that I have a little brother now, even though he is so much younger than me." Mark grew up with his two sisters.

"My mom has been the coolest through all of this. She understands that I want to spend time with my dad. In fact, she wants my sisters and me to go spend time with my dad." Mark went on to explain how through text messages, e-mail, and Skype, he is able to talk with his mom, dad, sisters, and half brother. Much of the time Mark initiates the conversations with his parents. "Since I do not come home that much, I love keeping in touch with them," he told us.

Mark's story illustrates how much he wants his family to be involved in his life. He mentioned that he keeps up with his aunts, uncles, and cousins on Facebook. The Millennials want a connected family, no matter how that family may look.

The Millennials are in the beginning stages of creating their own families. Most Millennials are not married, which is mainly because most Millennials are still young. Nonetheless, the expectations for marriage and children are high. I share the same optimism as my peers.

Family values may well become one of the main distinguishing marks of the Millennials. We believe that families will return to a point where we are no longer disconnected. This generation desires close family relationships, and we will make the effort to keep our families connected.

We want parental involvement. At first glance a connected family and parental involvement would appear to be similar. It would seem that if a family were connected, then a parent would naturally be involved. I would agree. But there is a distinct difference between a connected family and parental involvement for the Millennials. This difference is unlike any other generation.

Six out of ten Millennials look to their parents for advice and guidance. These 60 percent also told us that they receive a lot of advice from moms and dads. The majority of Millennials are not calling a parent just to talk. Millennials are calling parents to find out how to handle a disruptive coworker or how to approach the bank about a loan. Millennials want parental input about future career plans. This generation seeks the wisdom of their parents.

Given the autobiographical nature of this chapter, allow me to give another personal illustration. As stated earlier, I am not the typical Millennial. My main source of guidance and wisdom is Scripture. Beyond that, my wife is the one to whom I would turn for advice or counsel. Rachel and I talk about major and minor decisions that need to be made in regard to just about anything. So my main source of advice is not as common as other Millennials.

However, my wife would agree with the following statement: My parents are an extremely important source of advice for me. At times she might even jokingly say they are the most important source of advice! I understand why Millennial parents are the go-to source for advice. We know our parents have our best interests in mind; it becomes vague who else truly has our best interests in mind outside of close family and friends. Our parents also have a lot of experience. Additionally, today's decisions are not simple.

I value my parents' opinion very much. I am sure the 60 percent of Millennials who receive a lot of advice from their parents would agree with that statement. Because I value my parents' guidance, I would say they are the most influential people in my life. The majority of Millennials also stated that their parents are influential in their lives.

Nine of out ten Millennials stated they have been strongly influenced by their parents. The influence Millennials receive from their parents is largely positive. Millennials not only want parental involvement, but Millennials are receiving parental involvement. Parents are making themselves available to give the guidance and influence that Millennials desire.

The Millennial Generation may well be the most connected generation to their parents. Parents are involved in the weekly, if not daily, affairs of their Millennial children. Parents are staying involved with their children well into adulthood. And we want this! We want parental involvement.

We are diverse. Prior to the completion of the research, I had developed my own thoughts regarding the diversity of the

Millennials. My initial reaction to the diversity of my generation was "What's the big deal?" I realized I was thinking about diversity purely from personal experience. Diversity has always been a part of my life.

This diversity that Millennials are so accustomed to is extremely important. However, it needs to be viewed from a historical perspective to understand fully its significance. When looking at diversity from a historical perspective, the answer to "What's the big deal?" becomes much more important.

Previous generations made extra efforts to embrace those who differed from the majority. My dad has told me stories about the era of segregation, busing, and homogeneous friends. Both my dad and my mom grew up in the South at a time when racial differences were not accepted. Their generation, the Baby Boomers, saw diversity as an issue. Intentional efforts were made to create diversity during this time of major social change. Although all may not have agreed or liked the changes, the efforts were still made. Some saw the importance of intentionally including those of varying backgrounds, particularly those of different races.

Diversity is commonplace for the Millennials more than any previous generation. It is a nonissue. We have grown up in a world full of people from different racial and ethnic backgrounds. That explains my reaction to the issue of diversity. Previous generations have mandated and pushed for more acceptance and tolerance of differing ethnic and racial backgrounds. For Millennials diversity is a matter of fact. It is simply our reality.

The friendships made in the Millennial Generation reflect our diverse world. A majority of Millennials claimed at least some friendships with people who are different from them in race, lifestyle, age, and religious beliefs. Millennials have friends who look different, act different, and believe different.

We are not forced to have friends of varying backgrounds; instead these relationships naturally form regardless of race or ethnicity. Diversity is not an issue for Millennials. We do not feel a need to be diverse, and we do not seek out relationships for that purpose. It is just who we are. We are diverse.

We believe we can make an impact for the future. The Millennials are on the brink of taking on major responsibilities. Every year more Millennials are graduating from high school and college. Every year more Millennials are entering the workforce. Every year more Millennials are marrying. Every year more Millennials are having children. We understand the responsibilities that lie ahead of us. We are poised to make an impact for the future.

Nine out of ten Millennials believe it is their responsibility to make a difference in the world. As we continually move into adulthood, we are taking seriously the responsibilities given to us. Millennials understand ownership. We are not depending on those generations that preceded us or those generations that will follow to do what needs to be done. The presidential election of 2008 was largely decided by those who wanted change. Millennials spoke out regarding their desire for change, and their voice was heard.

Millennials are already beginning to think about how they can make a difference in the world. Three out of four Millennials believe it is their role in life to serve others. If 75 percent of Millennials begin to serve others, the impact for the future will be significant.

As stated earlier, I currently work in retail banking. My favorite part of my job is not making the big sale or landing the big client. Rather, I find joy when I help someone learn how to better handle his or her personal finances. I know this will make a more significant impact than putting them into the newest banking product. Seeing the look on an individual's face when he or she learns how to save more money or make more money is my favorite part of the job.

I work closely with three other Millennials, and we all seem to share that common desire to make a difference in the lives of our clients. This may well prove to be true of all of my coworkers. But I have noticed that my fellow Millennial coworkers tend to receive the most satisfaction from their job when they take extra effort to help a client.

In addition to Millennials believing it is their responsibility to make a difference in the world, six out of ten Millennials believe they will make some great contribution in their lifetime. We believe the world is at our fingertips. Parents have instilled a belief in us that we can do anything. Teachers have taught us that we can accomplish whatever we want as long as we put our mind to it. We not only have the belief that we can make a difference; we have the desire to do so.

The expectations for the Millennials are high, expectations that are self-imposed. While others may have helped guide our beliefs, we have taken them as our own. We believe we are going to accomplish great things. We believe we will make a significant difference in the world. We believe we can make an impact for the future.

We are not workaholics. "Would you like a 5 percent raise or an extra week of vacation for next year?" Aaron's boss presented this question to him. Aaron is a young professional working for a nonprofit organization in Kentucky. At the time of the question, Aaron was not sure about his answer. He recalled his thoughts to us: "The 5 percent raise would go a long way. I could pay off a lot on my student loans with the raise."

"But an extra week for me would be so nice," he reflected. "My brother and I have wanted to take a trip across the country. We've talked about it for years." Aaron was not able to answer his boss right away. He took several days to think about it. His boss, on the other hand, knew what Aaron would do.

Aaron's boss has some insight into this younger generation. He knew they moved from job to job frequently. He also knew they valued their personal time. He decided to present the option to Aaron thinking he would choose the vacation. It would end up saving the company money over the next year, and Aaron would probably move on soon anyway.

The boss was right; Aaron took the extra vacation week. He told us, "I knew I wouldn't be there long, so I took the extra week. The student loans were still going to be there in the next few years, but the trip my brother and I took was unforgettable."

The balance between work and life is the number one factor in job selection for Millennials. We want our personal time, just as Aaron did. A job that requires us to be on-call or working more than sixty hours is not appealing. Time spent with family and friends will take precedence.

These preferences should not indicate that we do not want to work. Previous generations may see us as lazy. The Baby Boomer generation typically works a lot. One of the defining characteristics of the Silent Generation is their hard work. Success was often defined by the amount of work completed. Millennials want to work. We are willing to work hard, and we know how to work smart. We just do not want to work long.

While a balance between work and life is important, a successful career is important as well. Millennials want to succeed. With the high expectations that were mentioned previously, we want to find work that will enable us to have career success.

However, we are not willing to obtain success at any cost. The Millennials' desire for success is tempered by their desire to make a significant contribution in their lifetime. Pouring all resources into a career does not fit our objectives. As we grow and excel in our chosen field, we continue to seek a way to make our mark on the world.

Our families and friends will not be forgotten as we pursue a career that demands all of our focus, time, and energy. We want to be with our spouses and experience the joys and sorrows of life together. We want our children to know their father and mother. The children we raise may well be the mark we leave on society.

The fact is we sometimes choose personal time over career advancement. The Millennials' view of success involves much more than a career path or a certain income. The proper balance of work and life is a must. We are not workaholics.

We want a mentor. Socrates, Plato, Aristotle, and Alexander the Great. You might be quick to notice three of the four are similar. Socrates, Plato, and Aristotle are all Greek philosophers. They spent their lifetime contemplating all aspects of life from philosophy to logic to arithmetic to science. They were masters of the mind. Engaging men in conversation was their passion. Their influences would impact societies and whole civilizations.

But what about Alexander the Great? Yes, he did impact civilizations but in a different way from the other three. Alexander was a world conqueror. His lifetime was spent becoming a master of the sword rather than the mind. Alexander the Great was known to be a military genius; he was both feared and respected.

Alexander would lead his men into battle by delivering the first attack on the opposing army. He was wounded numerous times but never lost a battle. His cause of death is unknown. Historians claim causes such as poison or typhoid fever.

There is a stark contrast between the lives of Socrates, Plato, and Aristotle and the life of Alexander the Great. Three of these men spent their lives sharpening the mind while one of these men spent his life sharpening the sword. But all four men have a common thread that runs between them. That thread is a mentor. Socrates mentored Plato. Plato mentored

Aristotle. Aristotle mentored Alexander the Great. All four men are seen as historic, powerful figures. Mentorship is powerful.

The Millennials understand the power behind a mentor. That is why we want one. Three out of four Millennials would like a leader to come beside them and teach them leadership skills. We value a leader who is willing to take his or her time to teach skills that otherwise may not be learned.

Desiring a mentor leads to the fact that we are teachable. Although we are confident, we are willing to learn. An experienced leader has value. Millennials understand this value, and we will listen to a mentor who has chosen to invest in us. However, we also want a mentor who is willing to listen to us.

A Millennial mentorship should have open lines of communication. A mentorship will only work if the mentor is available. A Millennial will expect the mentor to be easily accessible whenever we need him or her. With technology and social media, we have several avenues of communication, and we will use them all.

More than 40 percent of adult Millennials currently have a mentor in their lives. That means for every five Millennials, two are connected with a mentor. Those mentors are connecting to a generation that will be in leadership positions in the near future. Those mentors are influencing a generation whose children will be filling our schools. Those mentors understand the power of a mentorship. The opportunities to influence a generation through mentoring are abundant. We want guidance and advice. We want mentors.

We are green but not that green. Sustainable energy is energy that can meet the current needs of a population without possibly hindering the energy needs of future generations. Probably the greatest example of sustainable energy is solar power. The sun produces energy that can be harnessed and directed in ways we deem useful. While we use the sun's energy now, it will not affect a future generation's ability to also use the sun's energy. As the adage goes, "The sun will rise tomorrow."

Sustainable energy is a major focus for those who want to help maintain and restore our current environment. People are finding new ways to power their homes through solar power. Businesses are researching how to power vehicles using hydrogen or electric power. Wind turbines have increased in popularity in order to power towns and cities.

While the Millennials are pleased with these new innovations, we are not as concerned about the environment as most think. Millennials are not rabid when it comes to making the world green. Creating a clean and green environment is not at the front of our minds.

We understand the significance of doing our part for the environment. Millennials want to reverse the trends of previous generations. We believe that preceding generations caused harm to the environment. We are not certain of the reasons. It may have been because they did not know better or that they just did not care, but we believe those generations did not do their part to secure a healthy environment.

Although strong environmentalism is not a defining characteristic of the Millennial Generation, we will do our part. Millennials do not want future generations to say that we caused more harm than good to their environment. We will look for ways to help.

Many of us will proactively try to lower our carbon footprint. Some of us will spend extra time finding ways to eliminate unnecessary environmental waste. Still others will search for sustainable and renewable energies. Millennials will do our part to protect and restore the environment, but we are not obsessed with the issue. We are green but not that green.

We communicate unlike any other generation. Remember Mark? He provided us a firsthand look into his family life. You may have picked up on his methods of communication. He told us that he talks to his parents, sisters, or brother through text messages, e-mail, and Skype. He also mentioned that he keeps up with his extended family through Facebook.

Mark's situation is unique in the fact that his family members are choosing to communicate with him through those methods. What is not unique is Mark's using the multitude of communication avenues. While the previous insight may have been a surprise to you, this new information will probably not be a shock. Millennials communicate unlike any other generation.

Seven out of ten Millennials say the cell phone is vital in their lives. It is amazing that we use that term to describe our cell phone use: vital. Cell phones became available for public use in 1977. It was not until the 1990s that the cell phone market increased and it became a primary method of communication. Previous generations, with the exception of a few in the later years of Generation X, remember a world without cell phones. Millennials cannot say the same. Our world has always included cell phones.

I remember my first cell phone. I was in middle school, probably in eighth grade. It was a small Nokia phone with interchangeable faceplates. Many of my classmates had the same phone, and we were always comparing who had which faceplate. The phone stored up to a hundred phone numbers, had a couple of games included with the phone, most notably, a game called *Snake*. At the time an eighth grader with a cell phone was not the norm. Our age group was among the youngest to have a cell phone. I can only imagine what age group represents the beginning cell phone users now. Needless to say, I too would describe my cell phone as vital.

The pervasiveness of cell phones led to using them as the primary mode of communication for Millennials. The two most common forms of communication for Millennials are talking and texting on a cell phone. This explains why most Millennials say their cell phone is vital. We use our cell phones a lot! We do not go anywhere without them, and we monitor them constantly. We can always be reached if we want to talk to the person trying to reach us.

The most accessible way to reach a Millennial is by text. I text-message more often than I actually call someone. Text messaging is appealing. Millennials have learned to be brief in our conversation, eliminating the need to spend long amounts of time with other forms of communication. Text messaging gives the opportunity to choose your words without feeling the pressure of an immediate response. And it's easy. You do not have to find a quiet place or excuse yourself from a dinner table.

Texting is the primary method of communication for younger Millennials as well. Ask a member of the Silent Generation or even a large segment of the Baby Boomers how often they text. Do they use it more often than e-mail or a phone call? Although our research did not cover other generations, my best guess is that texting is not their primary form of communication. It is amazing that a technology about twenty-five years old has changed the way of communication for a whole generation. The Millennials communicate unlike any other generation.

We are financially confused. We have choices. If you go to the grocery store to pick up a jar of peanut butter, you will have to decide between smooth or crunchy. You have to decide between sodium-free, sugar-free, organic, and natural. Then there are the different brands: Jif, Skippy, Peter Pan, Reese's, and others. Which one do you choose? Living in a society with so many choices can make a simple decision complicated and leave a consumer thoroughly confused.

Millennials are feeling the effects of a consumer society when it comes to financial matters as well. Saving for retirement no longer means simply opening an account at the bank. Now there are options. Do you choose to place your money in a 401(k) or an IRA? What type of IRA: traditional or Roth?

Do you make investment decisions yourself, or do you pay someone to assist you? If you choose to have an investment advisor, which financial institution is the best? I could continue to play this scenario out, but I think I made my point. With so many choices and conflicting advice, Millennials do not know where to begin financially.

In order to eliminate confusion, Millennials are turning to the government for help. Almost seven out of ten Millennials believe the government should provide for their retirement. Millennials see a portion of their paycheck going toward Social Security and believe that they will receive help in return upon retirement. With the first Social Security check issued in 1940, Americans have received retirement help from the government for more than seventy years.

While most Millennials believe in government-supplied retirement income, we also believe that making a high income is important. Our expectations of success lead to expectations of a high salary. You can already begin to see where Millennials are financially confused. Obtaining a high salary usually equates to having a comfortable retirement with any government assistance being a nice bonus. Millennials, however, don't see it as a bonus. There is an expectation that the government will supply them with needed funds for retirement.

Throughout the research, we found conflicting and confusing answers to many of our financial questions. In response to a specific question on how confused Millennials are about financial matters, four out of ten stated they are financially confused. The answers given to other questions indicate many more are also confused. As we dive into the research later on in the book, you will see that we are indeed financially confused.

We are not religious. If there is one distinct difference between the average Millennial and me, it is religion. Millennials are the least religious of any generation in modern American history. Millennials are still spiritual. Three out of four Millennials say they are spiritual but not religious. If you state you are spiritual, most people will take that at face value. If you state that you are religious, you will have to define what you believe. Most Millennials are unable to define their beliefs.

In addition to the lack of religious clarity, Millennials are not participating in activities that are normally deemed religious. This is another side to only 75 percent of Millennials defining themselves as spiritual. Millennials are not involved with an established religion.

Sixty-five percent of Millennials do not regularly attend worship services. Saturday night is extending into Sunday morning. Millennials who are leaving home are also leaving church. As my generation is no longer in the habit of going to worship services on a regular basis with their family, they now choose not to go.

While only one out of three Millennials attend worship services regularly, only one out of five is involved with a small-group Bible study. Millennials are no longer choosing to identify themselves with religion. Most of my generation has decided to remain content with calling themselves spiritual.

Again, I must be clear about my bias. I am one of this generation who does not fit well with the majority data about religious preferences. While the statistics are trending in the opposite direction than I would like, I am encouraged by those Millennials who choose to remain faithful to their beliefs. I am privileged to have close friends who understand the importance of Christianity and have dedicated their lives to serving God. I believe these Millennials will make a tremendous impact in our generation. We will have to have an answer and reason for our beliefs. We will have to define why we are religious. Our peers will ask us. Our peers will question us. Our peers, the Millennials, will want to know why we believe what we believe.

A Millennial and the Older Guy

When the two of us collaborated on this project, we pledged that we would approach the data with as little bias as possible. We knew it would be hard to separate our evangelical beliefs from the interpretation of the data. But we have tried.

In this chapter I have shared with you my perspective on my generation, which clearly includes the worldview I hold. As we enter into the next chapters, you will see a fairly objective perspective on the Millennial Generation. Only in the last chapters do we enter into discussions with our religious beliefs at the forefront.

Again, welcome to my world, the world of the largest generation in America's history. From this point forward, we will include the older guy, my dad, in the discussions. But I have cautioned him that if he strays too far from accurately interpreting my peer group, I will bring him back in line.

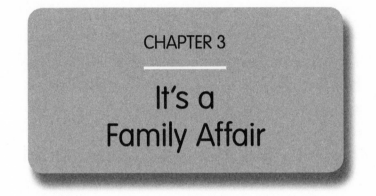

CHAPTER 3

It's a
Family Affair

G ee Wally, that's swell."

The quote is easily recognizable for many of you. It reminds you of a simpler time. But few people still use words like *gee* or *swell*. It is a language that is foreign to younger generations. The quote comes from Theodore "Beaver" Cleaver. Wally is his older brother. Wally and Beaver are the two sons of June and Ward Cleaver in the television show *Leave It to Beaver*.

The Cleavers are one of America's most famous television families from the 1950s and 1960s. The Cleaver family was depicted as a middle-class family living in a suburban neighborhood. The show's perspective was often from that of Beaver, who always found himself in some type of trouble. Many of the show's famous lines come from Beaver trying to work himself out of these troublesome situations.

June and Ward had the classic American marriage in the 1950s. A working father and a stay-at-home mother spent their free time rearing their children and discussing parental issues. June and Ward's loving marriage was a contrast for many real-life families who found themselves in poor relationships or problems with alcohol. The Cleavers' devotion to each other and to their two sons idealized marriage for many of the show's viewers.

American television produced many famous fictional families. These television families often represent the changing demographic of American families. The 1960s television family that caught the interest of most television viewers was the Clampett family. The Clampett family was quite a shift from the Cleaver family. The television show, *The Beverly Hillbillies*, provided a typical "fish out of water" setting. The Clampetts were a country, low-key, and moral family who relocated to Beverly Hills, California, after coming into a large fortune. Their family played opposite the self-indulgent, materialistic culture of southern California.

They were also one of the first television families without the typical husband-wife combination. The father, Jed Clampett, was a widower left to raise his daughter and nephew with the help of his mother-in-law. The 1960s family was still dominated by traditional family values, but subtle changes in the American family began to surface.

The Cosby Show is often described as the biggest television hit of the 1980s. The show's star, Bill Cosby, was the patriarch of an African-American family living in Brooklyn, New York. The show centered around a family with two working parents. Cliff Huxtable was an obstetrician, and his wife, Claire Huxtable, was a practicing attorney. Cliff and Claire raised five children in the midst of their successful careers. They dealt with their children's issues ranging from dyslexia to the teenage pregnancy of a friend.

The Cosby Show was unique in the fact that the show did not draw attention to the predominantly African-American cast. Issues of race were seldom addressed. The show did promote the culture of African-Americans in a positive light. In addition to more openness to racial issues, *The Cosby Show* also introduced the working mom into the American family. Moms were no longer viewed as homemakers as in previous generations.

By the 1990s television sitcoms dealing with families became popular. *Home Improvement, Family Matters, Full House, Frasier,* and *The Fresh Prince of Bel-Air* became highly popular as television sitcoms. Each presented a unique perspective on family.

One show that had a unique portrayal of the American family was *Married with Children*. The show's husband and father, Al Bundy, sells women's shoes and is stuck in the glory days of high school. He is pitted against his wife, Peggy Bundy. She spends most of her time watching television and taking Al's money for shopping sprees. Their daughter is a dumb, promiscuous blonde. Their son shows promise but is often distracted by his desire for women.

Married with Children may not depict the typical 1990s American family, but it does portray the moral decay that took place in American culture over the previous forty years. The difference between the families of *Leave It to Beaver* and *Married with Children* is significant. The American family is indeed different today from the American family of the 1950s.

The American family will continue to change. The Millennials are the next generation that will set the course for America's families. They have already learned a lot from their parents. And most likely their parents will continue to teach them.

Parents of the Millennials

The Millennial family begins with their parents. It is tempting to say that the Millennial family ends with their parents as well, but that might prove to be a stretch. Millennials' parents have played—and will play—one of the most pivotal roles in the shaping of the Millennial family. Let's take a quick look at the key characteristics of the majority of the Millennials' parents, the Boomers:

- Born between 1946 and 1964
- Second largest generation in American history
- Key events include the Vietnam War and Woodstock
- Early mentality of self-centeredness
- Became materialistic and demanding

The Boomers wanted the best for themselves. As the Boomer Generation began to have children, they wanted the best for their children as well. Their self-centered mentality eventually shifted toward meeting the needs of their children. The Boomers wanted everything to be perfect for the Millennial children. This attitude would prove to have lasting effects.

The Boomers have been watching over almost every element of their children's lives. Their constant hovering over the Millennials is sometimes compared to a helicopter hovering over people below. Hence, the parents of the Millennials are often called "helicopter parents." This connection between the Millennials and their parents is attributed to two main factors. The first factor, naturally, is parental involvement.

Parental involvement. The helicopter parents are more connected to their children than earlier generations. They opened all lines of communication and are available to their children at all times. In addition to being available, they will intervene as they deem necessary. They will make sure their children are as successful as they want them to be.

Helicopter parents want to give their advice in order to help prevent their children from failing. When we asked the Millennials just how many of them receive advice from their parents, the response was extremely high. Eighty-nine percent of Millennials receive guidance and advice from their parents. Parents of the Millennial Generation are involved with the affairs of the children. The Boomers are helping the Millennials make decisions about work-related issues. The Boomers are providing relationship advice to the Millennials. The Boomers are giving advice about future plans. The Boomers are extending their reach beyond their own generation to the lives of the Millennials.

Ron Alsop, author of *The Trophy Kids Grow Up*, states just how involved parents of the Millennials are when it comes to the workplace. Alsop notes:

> Strange as it might seem to older generations, the workplace is becoming a family affair. Companies today aren't just hiring the child; they get the whole family in the bargain, like it or not. Parents are getting involved from the start of their children's careers, bugging recruiters to schedule interviews, then asking to sit in on the job interviews, and even trying to negotiate salaries. The bonds are so tight that some corporate recruiters are finding that Millennials prefer to work in a location near their family and friends and avoid long-term international assignments.[1]

So how do the Millennials view the advice from their parents? Eighty-seven percent of Millennials view their parents as a positive source of influence. Millennials are heeding the advice of the second largest generation in America.

I (Jess) mentioned previously that my parents are an important source of advice for me. After my wife (Rachel) and I have a conversation about a decision that needs to be made, she will often follow up with the comment, "Go ahead and call your parents." Rachel knows that I value my parents' input. She will often seek her parents' advice about an impending decision. In fact, we call each other's parents for advice!

The Millennials' responses to parental involvement are similar to Jess' comments. "I call my mom about every little detail," Kari told us. She married two years ago and is expecting her first child. Kari said she keeps in touch with her parents every time something happens with her pregnancy. "I just want [my parents] to know what is going on. Plus, they know what they are talking about. They did have four children."

"I use them as my personal consultants," Mike spoke of his parents. "Lately we have talked about my career plans. I just finished my masters, and I do not really want to leave the area. My parents think if I move to a larger city I will have more opportunities. But I just do not know right now."

The Millennials are receiving significant amounts of guidance and advice from their parents. Millennial parents have been involved all the time. As long as the Millennials allow it, they will continue to be involved. And that leads us to our second factor of the strong connection between the Millennials and their parents: attached children.

Attached children. A relationship requires the involvement of two parties. The helicopter parents could hover and give direction, but if the Millennials chose to ignore them, their efforts would be useless. The Millennials are listening. In fact, it goes beyond listening. The Millennials are seeking.

Seventy-seven percent of Millennials agreed that they seek their parent or parents' advice on a regular basis. Much emphasis is placed on the parents as being the initiator of involvement with the Millennial Generation. In fact, the Millennials are just as responsible for the parents hovering. Millennials want mom and dad to help them through the tough (and easy) decisions.

It is the life the Millennials have always known. Their parents are involved with their education. If a Millennial is not making the grades, parent-teacher conferences are set up to ensure proper educational development. The Millennials' parents are watching their kids fill out college applications (if not filling it out themselves). Parents are hoping all the extra-curricular activities they enrolled their child in will pay off in the form of scholarships. The Millennials' parents are dropping them off to employer interviews. They are conducting follow-up calls for the interviews as needed.

Why would the Millennials not want this type of involvement? This involvement has only produced positive results for the Millennials. Better education, better careers, and better salaries are results of parental involvement. The Millennials are accustomed to this life. They have no problem knowing that they have help. An attitude of complete independence is not characteristic of most of the Millennial Generation. They see no point in unnecessarily severing ties with their parents.

The Millennials view their parents as a positive and available source of advice. But we also wanted to know if Millennials would seek counsel from other generations.

Millennials' View of Older Generations

With the positive influence the Baby Boomer Generation has on the Millennials, it is a safe assumption to think the Millennial Generation would have a positive view of older generations. But just how far does that assumption go? Remember the Baby Boomer Generation's (those who have and are raising the Millennial Generation) view of authority? The Boomers were antiauthoritarian in nature. They had a self-centered mentality. The Boomers wanted it all and wanted it now.

Something changed from the Boomers to the Millennials. We asked our twelve hundred research participants to agree or disagree with the following statement: "I tend to have great respect for people in older generations." Their responses were overwhelming. Of the Millennials interviewed, 94 percent said they have great respect for older generations. Those who agree strongly with the statement totaled 50 percent. Those who agreed somewhat with the statement totaled 43 percent.

Indeed, something changed. Unfortunately that "something" is not quantifiable. We can speculate that the connection between the Millennials and their parents has led to a natural respect for older generations. In our interviews Tim spoke about his respect for older generations. "I have always respected my parents. They taught me early to call adults by their last name using 'Mr.' or 'Mrs.' as well. That could be because of where I grew up too." Tim continued, "So I guess that is where my respect for older generations came from."

The respect may come from the involvement of grand-parents, aunts, uncles, and other relatives. Our conversation with Alisha gave us this impression. "My immediate family is large. In addition to my parents, my grandma and granddad were at almost every event in my life. My aunts and uncles lived in the same town as us, so they were heavily involved."

Alisha paused for a minute as if she had a new thought. She continued, "Now that I think of it, my great-grandmother lived with us until I was in middle school. I really think that is why I love being around older generations. It reminds me of my time with [my great-grandmother]. Our family has always had such a strong connection."

Our next conversation gave us the impression the Millennials' respect could just be a unique characteristic of the generation. We were pleasantly surprised at the simple response of Luis. We asked, "Why do you respect older generations?" He answered by saying, "I don't have a reason not to." To Luis it seemed logical to provide respect. His response fits well the mentality of openness and acceptance of the Millennials.

There is not one answer to why the Millennials respect older generations. The responses from those who were interviewed point to a combination of reasons. Regardless of the reasons, the response is overwhelmingly indicative. More than nine out of ten Millennials have great respect for older generations.

Millennials and Marriage

A wedding is a significant event, but weddings have not always been that way. I (Thom) remember my wedding vividly. It was in a small country church in Loflin, Alabama. We had our close friends and family attend. I doubt more than one hundred people were present. The ceremony lasted for maybe thirty minutes. Our reception was held in my wife's aunt's home. There was no music and no dancing. Cake and punch were served.

I cannot talk about my wedding without mentioning the most important factor, my wife (Nellie Jo). While the ceremony was simple, my wife was beautiful beyond description. Nellie Jo's beauty filled the entire church when she walked down the aisle. How thankful I am for the day she said, "I do!"

Weddings have changed dramatically in recent years. Just as Thom described, the days of a simple ceremony followed by a small reception in the church reception hall are fading. The rise in wedding costs over the past few decades illustrates the growth of the wedding ceremony. Even in recent history the costs have dramatically risen. The average cost of a wedding in 2000 was around $20,000. In 2010 estimates for average wedding costs are closing in on $30,000.

While the Millennials are not the only generation currently getting married, they are playing a large role in raising the costs on the wedding ceremony. They clearly see the wedding as a significant event. So, what about the reason for the wedding:

the marriage? Let's begin to answer that question by looking at the Millennials' traditional view of marriage.

Marriage as usual. The Millennials are a young generation. Many of them have not even begun to think about the prospects of marriage. But other Millennials have been married several years and have more than one child. As a reminder, we interviewed only those born between 1980 and 1991. When asked about the marital status of the Millennials, 55 percent responded that they are currently single. Twenty-six percent of the Millennial Generation is currently married. Of those who are married, most were twenty-four years or older.

My (Jess') dad took the liberty to share his wedding experience. In order to give the contrasting experiences between the generations, allow me to state my experience as a married Millennial. Engaged during my junior year in college, I took any free time during my senior year to drive to see my fiancée to help plan the wedding. Rachel graduated a year and a half earlier.

During the planning process Rachel and I often found that we were focusing on the guests. How many to invite? How many will attend? How much food to feed them? The ceremony was filled with flowers and decorations. The reception had a buffet line, a dance floor, special lighting, and a disc jockey. The whole even took more than half a day.

At one point we sat down to talk about the wedding. We reminded ourselves about the reason for the ceremony. We came to the conclusion that no matter what happened, we were getting married on June 2, 2007. Nothing would take that away from us.

When our wedding day finally arrived, it was beyond description. It was a day filled with laughter, tears, and moments of reflection. I will always remember Rachel's beauty as she walked down the aisle. Most importantly, Rachel and I made a lifetime commitment to each other. We know that our marriage is truly "until death do us part."

How does the Millennials' view on marriage compare to Jess' belief that marriage is a lifetime commitment? We asked the Millennials to respond to the following statement: "It is likely that I will marry more than one time in my life." For those who responded, 86 percent disagreed that they will marry more than once! Let me say that again, 86 percent plan to marry once or not at all!

The Millennials outlook on lifetime marriage is encouraging. Their perspective comes at a time when divorce rates are higher than ever. Failing marriages have become commonplace. Millennials believe they will begin to reverse America's divorce rate.

The Millennials' belief in marriage is promising. Ultimately their actions will tell their true belief in marriage. With approximately one-fourth of the Millennial Generation currently married, marriages are still in the early stages. We still wanted to know how many in the Millennial Generation are currently divorced or separated. Of our twelve hundred respondents, 2 percent are currently divorced or separated. The percentage is small, but the number of Millennial marriages is relatively small as well. Will the Millennial mentality of marriage remain? Only time will tell.

2.   **The changing landscape of marriage.** I (Jess) had the privilege of being in the wedding of one of my best friends from college. He and his wife started dating about the same time as my wife and I. The three years that the two couples spent getting to know each other were part of my favorite times in college. I really never thought of their relationship as differing from the norm until I was out of college.

Their marriage is different from the typical American marriage since they are from different races. He is Caucasian with blonde hair and a pale complexion, while she is of Asian decent with both dark hair and a dark complexion. We would often joke about their future children's appearance because we were that comfortable with their relationship. The comfort level our group of friends had in college is part of the changing landscape of marriage occurring within the Millennial Generation.

The openness of mixed marriages is unique to the Millennials. As Jess described, his view is extremely different from previous generations at his age. We will present just a snapshot of the Millennials' view on mixed marriages since we have an entire chapter dedicated to diversity and the Millennial Generation.

The vast majority of the Millennial Generation sees nothing wrong with mixed marriages. Only 7 percent of Millennials said they disagreed on some level with mixed marriages.

When we asked the question about acceptance of mixed marriages, we decided we would take it to another level. We asked the Millennials to open up and tell us if they would personally be willing to marry someone from a different race or ethnicity. Eighty-seven percent said yes, they would be willing to marry outside their race. There is only a small percentage drop between those who say mixed marriages are acceptable and those who would willingly enter into a mixed marriage.

Millennials are more open to the idea of mixed marriages than any previous generation. This openness is encouraging. With such high numbers, it led us to ask one more question about mixed marriages. We asked those already married to agree or disagree with the following statement: "The person I married is of a different race or ethnic background from me." Of those married, 22 percent agreed with the statement. Roughly one out of five Millennial marriages is a mixed racial or ethnic marriage.

The increase of mixed relationships is changing the landscape of marriage. The Millennials' openness is also changing other relationships within their generation.

Domestic partnerships and same-sex marriages. In 2008 California passed a constitutional amendment that stated only marriage between a man and women is valid or recognized in the state of California. It is often referred to as "Proposition 8." The passage of Proposition 8 became one of the most controversial issues regarding same-sex relationships in recent history. Proponents and opponents of the proposition spent more than $80 million in campaign funding. It became one of the most funded political campaigns in history besides presidential races.

Same-sex marriage is a political hot topic. It has undoubtedly affected the Millennials' view on domestic partnerships and same-sex marriage. We began our inquiry of the Millennials' view by asking how many Millennials currently have domestic partnerships. Those who stated they currently have a domestic partnership totaled 17 percent.

Domestic partnerships do not have the influence traditional marriages have, according to Millennials. When asked about sources of influence, guidance, and advice, spouses consistently ranked higher as a source over a domestic partner.

In addition to domestic partnerships, we wanted to know the attitude of the Millennial Generation toward same-sex marriages. The statement presented to participants of the generational study was as follows: "I see nothing wrong with two people of the same gender getting married." Forty percent agreed strongly with the statement. Twenty-one percent agreed somewhat with the statement. Twenty-four percent disagreed strongly with the statement. And 15 percent disagreed somewhat with the statement. The majority of Millennials see nothing wrong with same-sex marriages.

The landscape of marriage will continue to change with the Millennials. Increased acceptance of both mixed-race and same-sex marriages will continue. The decisions the Millennials make regarding their own marriages will affect other generations. It will specifically affect their children. We thus asked the Millennials to tell us about their children, children who have already arrived and children who are yet to come. Their response is next.

Raising a Generation of Their Own

"That's crazy to think about," José told us. "I am not even married yet. I couldn't imagine having a kid of my own." José is a twenty-four-year-old member of his city council. His two-year term started last year. "I definitely want to have kids. I just think that it will come a little later in my life."

The question we asked José was to estimate how many children he believes he will have. His political career was on the forefront of his mind, so it took him a minute to think about his answer. "Let me think about this. I love my family. I want to have one of my own. So I think I would like to have three." We asked José for his rationale for the number he chose, "The reason I say three is because that is how many my parents have. I am the middle child. I have an older sister and a younger brother. It just seems like the right amount."

We asked Mollie, and the rest of the twelve hundred participants, the same question. "Two," Mollie said without any hesitation. She informed us that she and her husband already had a conversation dealing with this exact issue after having their first child. "Tell us your reasoning for having two children," we said. "Two is just the only number that makes sense to me," Mollie said with a smile.

"Please explain," we asked.

"I definitely do not want to have one child. I believe it is good to have more so they can play with each other and entertain each other. In my opinion, an only child tends to be spoiled, which is natural because he or she does not have to share anything." Mollie continued, "When there are three children, it starts to become too hectic. You have to manage all the extracurricular activities. A five-passenger car or SUV becomes too small. And then there is the added cost. It just costs more to have three children as compared to two [children]."

Mollie added one last statement, "And do not even get me started on having more than three children. That just blows my mind. These parents that have five, six, or seven kids are crazy. I'll just leave it at that."

José and Mollie have different reasons for the number of children they would like to have. Regardless of why they want to have the number of children they do, they envision families of a similar size. The other Millennials' answers were similar.

In response to our asking, "How many children do you believe you will have?" the largest percent of Millennials agreed with Mollie. Almost half (47 percent) of the Millennial Generation believes they will have two children. Twenty percent believe they will have three children.

Thirteen percent of the Millennial Generation believe they will not have any children at all. Those who believe they will have one child totaled 9 percent. Large families are not on the Millennials' radar. Only 7 percent believe they will have four children. And 4 percent believe they will have five or more.

Small families appear to be on the horizon for the Millennial Generation. Though they desire smaller families, this generation intends to be family oriented. Indeed we see early indicators that the Millennials will be involved with their children.

Let me (Jess) illustrate with a personal example. When Rachel and I found out that she was pregnant, we made a commitment to go to every scheduled doctor's appointment together. From the beginning Canon (our son) was *our* responsibility. We both wanted to learn as much as possible about how to properly care for our new son. While the fear of entering parenthood pushed us to learn, the desire to provide the best for our son was just as much a factor.

Rachel read numerous books on pregnancy and infant care. She and I would often read the latest blogs from new mothers and fathers (there is a plethora of blogs from which to choose). We sought the opinions of numerous parents about their experience entering parenthood. And my personal favorite was when we enrolled in a birthing class. This was not your typical Lamaze class. It was a five-weeklong process that included everything from touring the hospital to the first few months of child care. I learned more than I ever wanted to know about pregnancy, birth, and child care during those five weeks!

We also did a large amount of research on cribs, car seats, and any other baby item that our son would be using. Even with all of our preparation, amazingly we still did not feel ready to enter parenthood. I later learned that was a normal feeling.

Rachel and I were not alone in our preparenthood endeavors. The class in which we enrolled had a wait list. The blogs we perused had high-traffic volume. The books we read were best sellers. Others were taking part in the same parent planning methods. Many of these others were Millennials.

Apparently the Millennials are going to be involved parents. They learned it from their parents, the Boomers. The Millennial Generation may become even more involved with their children than the Boomers are now. The Millennials may not hover around like the Boomers. But they just might be hanging in the shadows of their children, walking with them every step of the way. These "shadow parents" will create families that will be connected unlike any other generation.

The Connected Family

Based on the responses in our study, the Millennial Generation is already connected with their immediate and extended family. They want involvement with their family. And they want that involvement to be reciprocal.

Millennials are making the effort to assure that family members stay in contact with one another. They use different avenues to make contact with family members. Three driving forces are behind the Millennials connecting to their families unlike any other generation. Let's briefly look at each of them.

The return to traditional values. The return of the television show *Leave It to Beaver*, does not appear to be on the minds of television network producers at the moment. The Cleaver family does not portray the typical American family anymore. The return of *Married with Children* would not grab the attention that it once did either, especially for the Millennial Generation.

But based on the response of the Millennials, they desire to see their families return to more traditional values. The traditional values with the Millennials begin with their commitment. Eighty-six percent of the respondents stated the desire to marry only once or not at all. That also means that the Millennials are taking marriage more seriously. They are not marrying with the hopes that it will work. They are marrying with the commitment to make it work.

The Millennials demonstrate their traditional values through respect. As mentioned previously, 94 percent of Millennials respect older generations. They respect their parents and their grandparents. They respect their aunts, uncles, and other relatives. Millennials have a renewed sense of respect for those who preceded them.

The Millennial Generation also respects their peers. Their openness towards those of differing ethnic or racial background is greater than any generation in American history.

Millennials will be involved with their children. The Millennial Generation learned the importance of parental involvement from their parents, mostly Boomers. This generation wants children, and they are planning for them now. And those Millennials who already have children show they are heavily involved in their lives.

Technology helps with communication. Technology is a glue that holds the connected family together. The Millennial Generation is often associated with technology, and rightly so. They have grown up with the Internet, cell phones, and social media. The Millennials use their knowledge of technology to enhance communication with family members.

I (Thom) believe the cell phone has single-handedly kept me in touch with my three sons. I know that my boys would find ways to communicate with my wife and me, but the cell phone has made communicating with them easy. My wife and I usually talk to each son at least once a week. There are times when we talk to a different son every day.

If we are not talking, we are texting. If we are not texting, we are typing e-mails. If we are not typing, we are tweeting. Our family finds ways to communicate. The recent rise in technology has made staying in touch all the easier. One of the more recent communication avenues my sons and I use is Skype. My wife and I love to see our grandson. Jess will often let us entertain Canon via Skype. I cannot wait to do the same for all my grandchildren.

Thom's perspective on communication fits many families with Millennial children. Millennials are introducing their families to ways to stay connected. Social media is pervasive among the Millennials. They use this new technology once again to stay in touch with family. With so many communication options, it almost becomes harder not to stay in touch than it is to stay in touch.

Breaking the broken family. Unfortunately many families and family members have gone through divorce, separation, or abandonment. While parental involvement is high for Millennials' parents, that involvement often comes at separate times for mom and dad. Several Millennials have seen the effects of broken families, as children are often unintentionally caught in the middle of arguments and disputes. The Millennial Generation wants to break the trend of broken families. As previously stated, 86 percent of Millennials want to marry once or not at all. "My dad is currently married to his third wife. He never was around from the beginning.

My mom has taken care of me my whole life," Julie told us. Julie is an only child. Her dad keeps up with her around her birthday and Christmastime. She began to show emotion when she told us about the situation.

"I just don't get it. I am his only daughter. If he would just make the effort to know what is going on in my life, it would mean so much." Julie continued, "I know his absence is his fault alone. He made the choice. I am not mad at him, I just wish he wanted to hear about my life."

After pausing for a moment, Julie continued to talk. "The biggest lesson I learned from my absentee father is that I will not repeat his choice. I don't want my children to have the same emotional issues that I have. I do not want my kids to have to sit and wonder why." Julie continued talking about her relationship with her parents. We continued to listen as long as she wanted to talk. We knew that our interviews would often engender many emotions, especially related to families.

Julie's words show just how much the Millennial Generation desires their families to stay in contact. Returning to traditional values, the numerous communication methods, and the desire to break the trend of broken families will push the Millennials to have connected families. The mythical 1950s family may not reappear, but the Millennial Generation will have a connected family that could at least have some similarities with June and Ward Cleaver.

The Most Important Thing

What is really important in your life? That was the open-ended question we asked the Millennial Generation. Any answer was acceptable. The Millennials were clear in their responses. With twelve hundred different individuals, you can imagine that almost every conceivable response was covered. Some Millennials responded to issues related to careers, video games, education, alcohol, and music. They were not limited to any one response. The Millennials could list as few or as many facets of life as they felt were important. As the responses were gathered, we discovered some commonalities.

We were able to categorize the responses into fifteen main topics. Three topics related specifically to the family. Out of fifteen topics, raising children was ninth on the list. Eleven percent of Millennials stated that raising children was important to them. A spouse or partner was listed as the fifth most important element of life to the Millennials. Approximately 13 percent stated a spouse or partner as important in life.

The last response was the most important aspect of life according to the Millennials. An overwhelming majority claimed this response as important. In fact, this was the only response that was mentioned by the majority of the Millennials. The most important aspect in life for the Millennials is family.

Sixty-one percent of the Millennial Generation stated family was really important in life. Friends were chosen as the second most important facet of life for the Millennial Generation.

Twenty-five percent of Millennials stated friends were important.

We want to take a moment to allow you to read some of the responses from the Millennials. While the following list is not exhaustive by any means, it gives you an idea of just what the Millennials are thinking. Read the responses closely and try to get a feel for the Millennial Generation. Here is the Millennials' response when asked what is really important in life:

- My family is important in my life because without them I wouldn't be alive.
- My parents, my husband, and friends. They are really the most important things to me in my life. I hope we all can have good health and a happy life.
- In my life, my family is really important. Not just my children, but my mom and my husband and siblings. All of them support me and make me a better person. It is important to me to be healthy.
- God, family, friends, love.
- I love my family and friends. I enjoy traveling the world with my wife. I enjoy photography and taking lots of pictures. I enjoy sports and music.
- Being successful so that I can take care of my family.
- Family is most important in my life. They are my support system, my happiness, encouragement, and friends. Education is extremely important to me, I think that far too many people take it for granted. Also, balance, strength, and doing what you love.

I want to work in a job where I know I won't make much money, but I will be fulfilled every day knowing that what I'm doing makes a difference.

- My religion, my family, continually working on self-improvement, serving people, and living a fulfilling life.
- God, family, friends are most important to me. I believe it's important to live a life of service and servanthood.
- Family.

The Millennials will bring a renewed focus back to the family. Parents will continue their involvement. Older generations will love the respect they are given from the Millennials. The Millennial Generation may very well reverse the trend of failing marriages with their dedication and commitment. Millennials will be heavily involved with their children. The Millennial Generation will remain a connected generation to their family. There is nothing more important to the Millennials than family.

1. Ronald Alsop, *The Trophy Kids Grow Up*, 77.

CHAPTER 4

The New Normal of Openness and Diversity

I (Thom) wish I could say that my life has always been one that showed no prejudices and that never judged a person by the color of his or her skin or ethnic background. But such is not the case.

I grew up in Union Springs, Alabama, a small town in the southeastern part of the state. Union Springs is about twenty miles from Tuskegee, forty-five miles from Montgomery, and ninety miles from Selma. Those three towns are historically linked to the Civil Rights Movement and to the world of African Americans in the United States.

In 1964 and 1965 African Americans in Alabama grew frustrated at the systematic denial of blacks to register to vote. Numerous attempts to register resulted in more than three thousand arrests, police violence, and economic retaliation. On March 7, 1965, some six hundred civil rights marchers left Selma heading toward Montgomery to protest their denial of these basic rights. But they traveled only six blocks before reaching the Edmund Pettus Bridge. There state troopers and local sheriff's deputies, who wielded billy clubs and tear gas, attacked the marchers. Many were severely beaten, and all were driven back to Selma.

That day became known as "Bloody Sunday." I was nine years old.

Such was the world where I grew up. I remember my father driving me by Dexter Avenue Baptist Church in Montgomery and telling me about its famous young preacher named Martin Luther King Jr. And though I don't know if it's my recollection or my father's retelling of the story, I have memories of my dad in an argument with our circuit judge named George C. Wallace. Of course, Wallace later became a multiterm governor of Alabama and a candidate for the presidency of the United States. He is most famous for his staunch stands for segregation of races.

It is more likely that I recalled my dad's telling of the story because I was not even six years old. But that is the world that shaped me and influenced me.

In my early years I really didn't think twice about going to segregated schools, or drinking from separate water fountains, or having separate waiting rooms at the doctor's office. That was my world.

But I do remember my uneasiness when integration began in my school when I was in the fifth grade. I remember how strange it seemed to have a black student named Henry Huffman in my class. And I remember trying to be nice to him but never developing a relationship that could truly be called a friendship.

After all, good white boys just didn't do things like that. That was my world.

Then I remember in my teen years when I began to see the evils of racism and prejudice. And I remember my anger toward the white population of my town, those who had, from my limited view, perpetuated the racism. But that was the world they knew as well.

For these reasons and more, racial and ethnic diversity will always be an issue for me. I made the transition from the acceptance of racism to an advocacy against it. It will always be a conscious part of my world.

A Tale of Two Worlds

His perspective seems so strange to me (Jess). I've heard my dad talk about the Civil Rights Movement and the culture of racism where he grew up. But his stories sound more like a history book than any reality I've known.

One of my first friends was named Femi Babalola. His family moved to the United States from Nigeria. In fact, as I look back to my childhood, racial and ethnic diversity have always been a part of my life. I have known no other world.

I remember Dad asking me if one of my friends was getting married to the Asian girl he was dating. I actually had to pause for a moment to think about his question. When I thought of my friend's fiancé, her ethnic background was not the first thought in my mind.

My generation is not naïve. We know racism still exists. We know that injustices still take place. But our world is so different from the world of the Baby Boomers. When I read about the racism and the Civil Rights Movement, particularly in the 1960s, it seems so distant. But my father was only a kid in that decade. From 1960 to 1969 his age was five to fourteen. I can understand how all of these events impact him so significantly. I can understand how a boy growing up in south Alabama was shaped by this world.

But it's not the world I know.

My generation hardly ever saw racial and ethnic diversity as an issue; we rather see it as normative. The Millennials rarely describe someone first by their skin color or by their ethnic origin. That's not what is at the foremost of our minds. For us ethnic diversity is normative. I even struggle with the title of this chapter, "The New Normal of Openness and Diversity." For me this is nothing new. It is the life I've always known.

But from the older coauthor's perspective, it is a new normal. It is a major change from the Baby Boomers to the Millennials.

So I will yield to the perspective of the old man.

A Richly Diverse Generation

The Millennials represent the most racially and ethnically diverse nation in America's history. This is also the generation with the lowest proportion of Caucasians. By 2000 nonwhites and Latinos accounted for more than one-third of the total population of the Millennials. That's nearly 50 percent higher than their representation in the Boomer generation, and nearly *200 percent* higher than that of the seniors born before 1946. The world of the Millennials is indeed different from that of their parents and grandparents.

The diversity is not just about their friends and acquaintances. It is about the family of the Millennials as well. One out of five Millennials has at least one immigrant parent. And one in ten of this generation has at least one noncitizen parent.

Neil Howe and William Strauss, in their early work on the generation, *Millennials Rising*, note that the racial and ethnic groups of the Millennials defy common stereotypes. Nonwhites are the most likely to have school uniforms. Schools of the nonwhites are most likely to impose back-to-basics academic standards. Nonwhites have the fastest decline in street murder, child poverty, teen pregnancy, and school violence. Nonwhites are more likely to have two parents in the household than a decade earlier.

The proportional decline among whites and the corresponding increase among nonwhites in the United States are incredible stories. In 1970, when the oldest Boomer was twenty-four and the youngest Boomer was six years old, whites accounted for 88 percent of the total population.

By 2008, when the oldest Millennial was twenty-eight and the youngest Millennial was eight years old, the proportion of whites in the total United States population had dropped to

65 percent. Among just the Millennials, whites account for only 60 percent of the total generation. The cultural impact of such a huge shift is immeasurable. But one thing we know for certain: the worlds of the two largest generations in America's history are dramatically different.

We were pleased that our survey of twelve hundred Millennials was representative of the total generational population in America. Keep in mind that we surveyed and interviewed the older portion of this population, those born between 1980 and 1991. Let us review again how this generation looks from the demographic perspective of our study:

- The age of our respondents was distributed almost evenly from birth dates of 1980 to 1991. The percentage in each year ranged from 7 percent to ten percent, except for the birth date of 1991, the youngest in our study, where the proportion was 4 percent.
- The split between male and female respondents was almost equal, 51 percent and 49 percent respectively.
- The race and ethnicity of the respondents closely mirrored that of the national population of Millennials: 61 percent White; 19 percent Hispanic; 14 percent Black, 5 percent Asian, and 1 percent other.

We risk boring you with these numbers so that you could see the growing diversity of this generation. It is little wonder that diverse races and ethnic groups are simply normative for those who grew up with this reality.

Mary and Shelly are best friends. They met each other at a state university and have remained close since. They were both born in 1984 and graduated from college the same year. Because of their close friendship, they both tried and succeeded in finding jobs in the Orlando area. They currently share the rent on a three-bedroom apartment, an arrangement that will soon end since Mary is getting married.

Mary's mother is an immigrant from Korea. Her father is white and was born in the United States. Both of Shelly's parents are white. Our interview covered several topics, but the slowest part of the discussion was about diversity. What was particularly fascinating was that neither woman mentioned the ethnic difference between them until we raised the subject.

"I never think about our ethnic differences," Mary said matter-of-factly. "I mean, I was born and raised in America. Yeah, my mom is a Korean, but most of my cultural influences are American. I am proud of my Korean heritage, but I just don't think in terms of racial or ethnic backgrounds."

Shelly quickly agreed: "I think of Mary as my best friend. I never think of her in terms of her ethnic background. In fact, it didn't register with me until you brought it up. We have always lived in a diverse world. I think the only thing that would seem strange to me would be if everyone around me were the same color and the same race. For me the diverse world is normal. Anything else is just weird."

Similarities between the Two Big Generations

The Baby Boomer generation, those born between 1946 and 1964, were the recipients of more recognition and publicity than any other in American history. Indeed, studies of generations were largely the work of academic tomes until the seventy-seven-million-member Boomer Generation became the subject of more popular works.

The sheer size of the generation fascinated both the writers and the marketers. And the marketers made a valiant effort to touch the self-centered nature of the Boomers. "Have it your way," one burger franchise declared. "Go for all the gusto you can get," a popular beer company insisted. "You deserve a break today," another fast-food chain suggested.

We are already noticing a wake-up call of many companies that are making bold moves to capture the attention of the Millennials. Once again the massive size of this generation warrants such attention. If one has goods to sell or services to offer, seventy-eight million is too large of a number to ignore.

Another similarity in the two big generations is their groundbreaking relationships with different races and ethnic groups. The Baby Boomers were expected to break the shackles of segregation. Many of them began their lives surrounded by people that looked just like them. But as they grew up, they became the first Americans who, to a significant extent, actually broke racial and ethnic barriers.

For this reason, Baby Boomers tend to be conscious of those of different colors and different backgrounds. And most

Boomers have become intentional about righting the wrongs of previous generations.

The Millennials took further steps. Their parents were highly intentional about matters of race and ethnicity. But the children of the Boomers have become a generation that crosses barriers naturally and with little awareness of their groundbreaking behavior. The Boomers tried to cross the barriers, sometimes succeeding but sometimes not. The Millennials are the true success story. Most of the members of this generation are truly color blind in the best sense of the phrase. They are taking racial and ethnic relationships to new levels.

Evidence of the Shift

In our interviews with the Millennials, we saw clear evidence of this shift in relationships across ethnic and racial lines. One reason is commonsense: 68 percent of the Millennials grew up in places that had significant diversity. "I can't ever remember a time when I was not in a mixed racial crowd," said Brooke, a twenty-three-year-old Millennial. "I've heard my parents talk about the segregated world they grew up in, and it just seems weird. It's hard to believe that was common in the United States just a few years ago."

Hector agrees. His parents moved from Mexico to the United States before he was born, so he's never known an all-Hispanic world. "I would never call my parents bigoted or racist, but to this day most of their friendships are with other

Mexican immigrants. Not so with me. I have friends from so many backgrounds because that's the world I grew up in."

Nonwhite Millennials were more likely to grow up in a racially and ethnically diverse world. Eight out of ten nonwhites affirmed that their world as children was diverse, while six out of ten whites did so. To some extent the level of education of Millennials was related to the diversity as well. Less educated Millennials were more likely to say they grew up with diversity.

So how does this generation that was raised in a racially and ethnically diverse world fare today? As one might expect, these young adults are developing relationships in much the same pattern as they were raised.

In our study we asked about the backgrounds of their friends. Did those closer relationships come from people more like you or less like you? The responses were intriguing. About 70 percent of the Millennials acknowledged a friendship with someone of a different ethnic or racial background. From our perspective this response is the true test of crossing barriers. The Boomer generation became the generation of tolerance, but the Millennials do not simply "tolerate" those of different skin colors or ethnic backgrounds. They are far more likely to embrace them as friends and to make them a part of their world.

But we did not limit our questions of openness and diversity to just race or ethnicity; we also asked questions regarding religion, age, and lifestyle. The responses again reflect the ease by which this generation interacts with others who are different from them. The same high number, 70 percent, say they have friends who have different religious beliefs. In chapter 10 we will examine this issue more closely. For now we can say that the Millennial Generation cannot be defined by any one religion or faith.

We further asked if they had friends who had different lifestyles from their own, and these responses were even higher. Though we didn't define "lifestyle" with specificity, 80 percent of the Millennials affirmed that their circle of friends included those who lived differently from them. Some of the respondents spoke of friends who had a different sexual orientation than their own. Others related the lifestyle issue to wealth or social standing.

Still others said that some of their friends had different lifestyles because of contrasting religious beliefs, an obvious indicator that our questions were not mutually exclusive. "I grew up in a nonreligious family," Todd told us. "But one of my best friends describes himself as a born-again Christian. We are good friends, but we really do have contrasting lifestyles. I guess you could call his lifestyle strict compared to mine."

Another indicator of the diversity of and acceptance by this generation is their relationship with those of other generations. Over three-fourths of the Millennials have a friendship with someone of another generation. Of course, the Millennials are the youngest adult generation in America today, so we can only presume that these friendships are with older people. Indeed some of the other questions affirm our presumptions. Let's look at this issue a bit more closely.

The Attitudes of a More Open Generation

The Millennials simply see many things differently from previous generations. As we indicated earlier, it would be wrong to see their openness as mere tolerance toward others. They have moved beyond tolerance and acceptance to acting upon their beliefs.

94%

Toward older adults. For example, we just mentioned the issue of friendships across generations. In one of the most overwhelming responses of the survey, 94 percent of the Millennials indicate that, to some degree, they have great respect for older generations. This response really caught the two of us by surprise. It may prove to be one of the most significant findings of this study.

I (Thom) remember well when one of the slogans of the Baby Boomer Generation was "Trust no one over thirty." Most of us believed that and lived it, at least until we turned thirty. Now our children are saying that some of their key friendships are with older adults. And they told us that those for whom they have the greatest respect are older adults. What a significant shift between the two largest generations!

But this makes perfect sense to me (Jess). As we saw in the previous chapter, Millennials tend to be close to their Boomer parents. That is certainly how I view my own parents. Many of us have never known a time when we didn't have a close relationship with someone older than us. Yeah, our parents were sometimes "helicopter parents," hovering over us in matters of the smallest details. But we knew that they loved us, that they were looking after our best interests, and that we could talk freely at any time. It is little wonder that today we have a healthy respect for older adults.

We tried to discern a pattern among different subgroups of Millennials, but the only pattern we found was consistency. Respect for older adults crossed gender lines, racial and ethnic lines, and religious lines. No matter where we looked in this generation, we found a healthy respect, if not admiration, for older adults.

It is indeed a different world.

Toward mixed racial/ethnic marriages. I (Thom) have clear memories of my white cousin marrying an African-American man when I was thirteen years old. It was the scandal of the decade in my hometown. I recall two distinct reactions. The first type of reaction came from the outspoken critics who couldn't stop talking about it. Of course, many of their comments were laced with racist words and phrases. The other reaction came from those who refused to speak about it in any way. It was as if their silence meant that the "problem" did not exist.

I wish I could say that I had no issue with the marriage, but such was not the case. I was highly influenced by the culture of the deep South and residents of my hometown. Unfortunately I still remember anger toward my cousin that she would do such a thing.

But the times are surely changing.

And the Millennials are leading the way. When we asked them if they saw anything wrong with two people of different races or ethnic backgrounds getting married, an overwhelming 93 percent said no!

"I don't get it," said Kevin, a white twenty-four-year-old from Minnesota. "It's just skin color. Why do older people get so upset about it? It just makes no sense to me. Look, I've known many times when two white people marry, they have a ton of trouble. They're not compatible so they get a divorce. Two people with different skin color can have more in common than two with the same skin color."

Again, subgroups of Millennials have the same attitude as the generation as a whole. Mixed marriages by race or ethnicity are simply not a problem for these young adults regardless of gender, race, ethnic background, or religious preferences.

Millennials also expressed a willingness themselves to be married to someone outside their racial or ethnic group. Nearly nine out of ten, 87 percent, expressed this attitude.

Interestingly, when we asked the married Millennials how many of them had actually married outside their racial or ethnic group, only 22 percent said they had done so. Still, nearly one out of four is a high number by historical standards. With the open attitude expressed by the Millennials, we will not be surprised if that number increases in the years ahead.

Toward same-sex marriages. The Millennials are definitely more open to same-sex marriages than predecessor generations. Six out of ten expressed no concern about homosexual marriages, but the number was only four out of ten who were strongly supportive.

This is one of those issues that has significant variation among subgroups. Men, African-Americans, and residents of the South were considerably less comfortable with same-sex marriages than other subgroups.

As one might expect, though, the greatest variation came from religious subgroups of this generation. For example, if the Millennial did not attend church, he or she was in a group where 74 percent are supportive of same-sex marriages. An even higher number, 85 percent, of those who said they have no religious background were in favor of homosexual marriages.

But the numbers decrease dramatically when a Millennial labeled himself or herself "Christian." Barely a majority, the number supporting same-sex marriage drops to 51 percent. As we will note in chapter 10, the self-label of "Christian" applied to those who may have no commitment to historical Christian beliefs, but who say it's the closest religious term for them.

When we began defining Christianity by a series of questions that we labeled the "born-again" group, the number supporting homosexual marriages dropped dramatically again to 26 percent. And when we further defined the Christian faith to basic core doctrinal beliefs, the number in favor of same-sex marriage dropped even more to 16 percent.

At this point we can make two conclusions about the Millennials and their openness to same-sex marriage. First, they are more supportive than any previous generation. Second, the closer one holds to the historical and doctrinal tenets of Christianity, the more he or she would be opposed to homosexual marriages. The culture wars are not yet over on this issue, but those who are open to same-sex marriages have made significant gains with this generation.

Hank is an African-American born in 1982. He is also a Christian, defined by our strictest parameters in the study. He is unwavering in his opposition to marriage by two people of the same sex. "This is not a cultural preference, you know," he began. "This is about choosing absolutes. The Bible is crystal clear that homosexual behavior is wrong. There is no way we should ever think of condoning homosexuals getting married. I'm not homophobic like some people have accused me, and I don't think homosexuality is the unpardonable sin. But I know if you really believe the Bible, you can't condone it."

Ellen is a Caucasian born in 1982, the same year as Hank. She chose "no religion" as the best way to describe her religious beliefs. She sees people like Hank as imposing their beliefs on others. "Look," she began in a calm voice, "I don't tell other people how to live their lives. I don't impose a standard of morality on them. It is beyond me to comprehend why some people insist on telling others how to live and whom to marry. It makes no sense at all."

Returning to our original discussions about Millennials and same-sex marriage, recall that six out of ten were supportive. It becomes self-evident, then, that the number of Christians among the Millennials is small because they do not tip the scales in favor of opposing same-sex marriage. In fact, the number of Christians is the lowest percentage in over a century. We will look at that issue in detail in chapter 10.

Toward multiple marriages. Much has been said about the divorce rate in America, and the number of people who will marry more than once. So how do the Millennials feel about divorce and remarriage? In light of the previous discussion on same-sex marriage, their responses are somewhat surprising. On this issue they actually take a more conservative turn.

Despite the dire marriage statistics this generation faces, the Millennials remain both optimistic and determined to make marriage work. And because of the broken homes they experienced, this generation is committed to making marriage work. We heard about this hopeful note in the previous chapter.

Recall that few Millennials actually believe that they will marry more than once. In fact, the number is overwhelming: 84 percent of this generation believe they will not marry more than one time. A few who responded to our question doubt they will marry at all. But the reality remains that for over eight out of ten Millennials, divorce is not considered an option.

Of course, we understand that belief and action are not always the same, but the attitude to make marriage work in this generation is extremely healthy. Indeed, family is the Millennials' number one priority, including their determination about marriage. The previous chapter painted an encouraging picture about this generation and the family.

Some of the Millennials were certainly reacting to their own home life as a child and teen. "I love both my mom and dad," Renee said with total sincerity. "But I don't think they realize how painful divorce is for the children. Dad moved out when I was twelve years old. I thought my world was coming to an end. And then he moved three states away and remarried. It was miserable to get on a plane once a month to spend a weekend with Dad. It's not that I don't love him or want to see him; it's just the constant moving around was depressing."

Renee paused for a moment. She then continued with a look of fierce determination in her eyes. "I am not getting a divorce, ever," she said emphatically. "I have been married two years, and I told my husband that I will kill him if he ever leaves me. The good thing is that he's not sure if I'm joking or not."

Okay, we're not advocating murder as the punishment for divorce, and we knew Renee used the extreme illustration to make a point. But we have no doubt from our interview with her that she meant the rest of her words literally.

"I sometimes can have real anger toward my parents," she told us in a quiet and somber tone. "I just know they could have tried harder to make the marriage work. And I sometimes think they were selfish. They put their own needs and emotions before their children. I'm just not going to do that."

Dan has a similar attitude as Renee, but his story is different. His parents are still married. Both seem happy. And both have always seemed committed to their marriage.

"I'm not blind to their faults," Dan told us. "Both Mom and Dad have pretty hot tempers, and they didn't always keep their arguments and fights private. But I really never had any doubt they loved me," he said with certainty.

Yet Dan saw so many broken marriages that he pledged he would not be one of those statistics. "I've got so many friends whose parents are divorced," he said. "I've heard their stories about how difficult it was. Some were a part of blended families. Others had to spend time at two different homes, sometimes in different cities. I'm not going there, not for my marriage or for my kids."

The remarkable part of Dan's story is that he was just eighteen years old when we interviewed. He represented the youngest Millennial in our study. And Dan has no one that he is dating regularly. But he's already planning for marriage. And the marriage for which he's planning will be the old-fashioned, "till death do us part."

As we began to dive deeper into the responses about marriage, we saw some fascinating trends. First, all subgroups we studied had an adverse view of multiple marriages. As a reminder, many of our questions were asked using a form of the Likert scale. In the question about multiple marriages, the four possible responses were strongly agree, agree, disagree, and strongly disagree.

When we thus made the statement, "It is likely that I will marry more than once," the two categories of disagree and strongly disagree were the responses of *more than 80 percent in every subgroup*. The aversion to divorce and remarriage was clear. But when we looked at the "strongly disagree" category, differences emerged. Christians were more likely to respond, "Strongly disagree." And those Christians who held to more historic and biblical tenets of the Christian faith were even more likely to disagree strongly.

Not necessarily what you expect. The attitudes of the Millennial Generation defy any neat categorization. They are certainly open to diversity among races and ethnic groups. Perhaps it's better to say diversity is normal for them; anything else seems strange.

Likewise, this generation has a great attitude about relationships with older adults. As we saw in the previous chapter, this attitude seems to stem from the overall healthy relationships they have with their parents.

It is unlikely that the often-heated discussion about homosexuality and same-sex marriage will go away with this generation. Still, there is a definite shift more open to both with the Millennials. On this particular issue we saw significant variances among the subgroups.

While the issue of sexuality is trending more liberal, the issue of divorce and remarriage is trending more conservative. Then again, this attitude is not a huge surprise in light of our earlier discussion on the family in chapter 3.

The Big Four Factors

As we reviewed the data and interviews on matters of diversity and attitudes, four common factors, or themes, emerged. And, like the overall study on this generation, the perspective is generally positive with some exceptions.

The progress of previous generations has benefited the Millennials. Today's young adults are largely color-blind. They often think it's silly to focus on such issues as race and ethnicity. Hillary, a twenty-seven-year-old Arkansan, commented, "I know racial issues were really important in previous generations. I'm not blind to the history of the Civil Rights Movement and other big issues. But I don't think of skin color any more than I do what size feet someone has."

Hillary is right on both counts. Race and ethnicity were and are big issues for previous generations. And she rightly gives credit to her elders for the progress that has been made. "I remember studying about some of the heroes of the Civil Rights Movement of the sixties," she told us. "I realize that many who have gone before us deserve the credit for the great progress we've made."

Typically the Millennials point to the Baby Boomer Generation when they give credit for the advances in racial and ethnic relations. They point to the protests and social upheaval of the sixties and naturally think of the Boomers during that era. The reality, however, is that many of the leaders, Martin Luther King Jr. for example, were not Baby Boomers but belong to the World War II generation. King, for example, was born in 1929, well before the first Boomer was born in 1946.

Still, the overall thesis that Millennials benefited from previous generations is valid. Most of those we interviewed recognized this reality and demonstrated appreciation for the work of those born before them.

The Millennials have reacted to the marriage failures of their parents. The conventional wisdom is that the American divorce rate is around 50 percent. There seems to be no solid evidence to support a number this high. The more consistent research asserts that the divorce rate among Boomers and the World War II generation is in the 32 to 38 percent range.

Still, the societal and family impact of at least one in three marriages ending in divorce is significant. The Millennials are clearly reacting to these failed marriages. Even if their own parents remained married, they all know someone close to them who has been impacted by divorce.

We do not have to speculate about this reaction. The Millennials clearly told us that they were determined to have healthy marriages, unlike their parents or many parents in the Baby Boomer generation. Multiple interviews provided us this consistent theme.

We should not be surprised. Many Baby Boomers reacted to the more distant relationship they had with their parents. As a consequence, they were determined to have a close relationship with their own children, the Millennials. And that issue brings us to the third of the big four factors.

3. **Parental influence is huge in this generation.** This factor may seem self-evident for any generation. After all, what generation hasn't been impacted by their parents, for good or bad? We see three specific issues with the Millennials and their parents, and they are mostly positive.

First, the level of intergenerational conflict is modest. The Millennials are able to direct their emotions and energy into more positive directions. Perhaps that at least partially explains why this generation is more service oriented than their predecessor generation.

Second, as we saw in the previous chapter, many Millennials see their parents as both friends and advisors. In some cases the parents were "helicopter parents" to their Millennial children. They hovered over them to an extreme and a fault. Some parents continued that behavior when their children reached adulthood.

Overall though, the close relationship between parents and children has proved healthy. The Millennials certainly have someone they can call in time of need.

Third, because they are so close to their parents, many Millennials have a respect and admiration for older adults in general. This younger generation is comfortable in a setting of mixed generations, and they often speak of their elders with deference and respect.

Christians in this generation tend to have different views on some issues. Perhaps one of the more amazing insights we gleaned on matters of diversity and openness is how consistent the views are as we look at different subgroups.

On most issues of diversity and openness, the Millennials spoke in near unanimity. The responses were consistent across the age spectrum, in all races and ethnic groups, in all socio-economic groups, and in all religious groups.

The group that showed some variation on two issues was Christians. First, Christians had stronger agreement on the matter of staying married to only one person. Second, they had less openness to accepting the homosexual lifestyle.

We will delve into religious issues of the Millennials in chapter 10. For now we will simply repeat that the stronger the Christian commitment, the stronger the view on matters of divorce and homosexuality. We will look at many of the implications of religious preferences in chapter 10.

Overall a Good Report

Though some will express concern about the Millennials and their views on diversity and openness, the report overall is good. Many will applaud their color blindness toward those of different races and ethnicities. Some will have concerns about the helicopter parents, but most will be pleased that this generation has such healthy relationships with their mothers and fathers.

Most will be gratified that the Millennials as a whole have a commitment to stay in one marriage. Of course, the skeptic will insist on a wait-and-see approach. He or she will not be satisfied with the intentions of this generation.

And there is significant evidence to tell us that the Millennials will cross generational lines with little problems. Contrary to the attitudes of their parents in earlier years, this generation does not view older adults with enmity.

"I'm really glad I'm a part of this generation," Zach said with a smile. "I like how we are the generation that has such great relationships with people who look differently or have another ethnic background. I think we have a real opportunity to make a difference for the good. I think the world could be a better place because of us in twenty to forty years. I say that hopefully and not arrogantly."

Zach represents many in his generation who are really motivated to make a difference. That issue of motivation with the Millennials is fascinating. What really makes them tick? We'll answer that question in the next chapter.

CHAPTER 5

Motivating the Millennials

Those were the good old days.

We like to be nostalgic. We like to think about the days before automobiles, jets, computers, and countless amenities.

Those were simpler times. Those were times when the family unit stayed intact. Those were the times when your grandparents lived near you and you had the same neighbors for life.

Though we never lived them, we long for the good old days.

But we tend to forget some convenient facts about those good old days. Medical advances were so far behind those we enjoy today. Let's say you choose 1850 as a pinpoint for the good old days. You probably would not have lived too long to enjoy them. Your life expectancy at birth was thirty-eight years.

Okay, let's fast-forward a half a century to 1900. As the twentieth century dawned, certainly life was better and simpler. Or was it? Life expectancy was certainly higher fifty years later, but you wouldn't be expected to reach fifty years old. And the top three probable reasons for your death would be pneumonia, tuberculosis, or diarrhea. By the way, if you had any noticeable mental illness or if you had tuberculosis, you were sent and segregated into a sanatorium. You then could no longer participate in the larger community and live a normal life.

The good old days? Hardly.

What is appealing about those days is the simpler life they represent. The hectic and frenzied pace most of us live has us longing for something different, something slower, and something more meaningful.

The Millennials may be the first generation to capture the best of the good old days. They may represent a huge shift in the way the American adult views priorities and life. Sure, these young men and women have dreams like those of previous generations, but those dreams alone are insufficient.

One of the goals of our study of twelve hundred Millennials was to try to understand what makes them tick or what motivates them. We looked at family issues, religious issues, and workplace issues. We looked at a wide spectrum of economic issues, particularly how they are driven by careers and money. We examined concerns about personal health and to whom they turn for help.

We probed even more to learn what the ultimate goals and dreams are of this generation. And we even asked about the role they saw the government playing in helping them fulfill their goals and dreams.

In this chapter we will look at how Millennials are motivated. What excites them and gives them drive? What are the sources of hope and their greatest fears?

The Millennials may not have lived in the days when families rarely moved and when relationships were largely stable, but they seem to be moving back in that direction. Though they may still be highly mobile, these young men and women are determined to stay connected in relationships. And with the wide availability of technological devices that allow them to do so, they may truly become the relationship generation.

It's All about Relationships

Thom and Jess live 550 miles apart. In an earlier generation, such a distance would have limited communication options. The drive was too long; the flight was too expensive; or the long-distance rate was too costly. For example, when Thom kept in touch with his widowed mother several years ago, they each took turns calling on alternating Saturdays. Their budgets could only handle two long-distance calls a month each.

The options have certainly changed today. For one, Jess has never had a land telephone line. He calls Thom on his cell phone at no cost beyond the fee he pays for his monthly plan. The call to Thom is at no incremental cost.

Thom and Jess also stay in frequent contact by e-mail, by Twitter, by text messaging, and Jess is a regular on Facebook.

When Jess and his wife Rachel gave Thom and Nellie Jo their first grandchild, Canon, the mode of communication began to include Skype so they could see that grandson via live video on their computers. And amazingly, every form of communication mentioned in this paragraph is free.

The danger in listing these forms of communication is that the pace of technological change will quickly bring new approaches and this book will seem dated!

Further, when Thom and Nellie Jo can't be satisfied just seeing their grandson on Skype, they aren't hesitant to get on a flight from Nashville to Raleigh on Southwest Airlines. Rates are highly affordable.

But the most fascinating part of the communication line between Jess and Thom is Jess' desire to stay in touch with his mom and dad. He will often initiate the communication; and it's not unusual for him to contact his parents several times a week via cell phone, text message, e-mail, Twitter, and Skype.

Jess is a typical Millennial in this regard. He values relationships, and he is determined to do his part to keep relationships open and active.

We cannot overstate how important relationships are in motivating this generation. We asked the open-ended question, "What is really important in your life?" The respondents could have listed any number of choices. The results are amazing.

"Family" was the overwhelming response, noted by 61 percent of the Millennials. "Friends" was a distant second at 25 percent. And, much to our surprise, no other response was greater than 17 percent.

In chapter 3 we shared with no equivocation how important families are to Millennials. With friends as a second choice in importance in life, we learned quickly that relationships motivate and drive this generation.

1   The best motivators in the workplace for this generation are relationships.

2   The best connectors in religious institutions are relationships.

3   The best way to get a Millennial involved in a service, activity, or ministry is through relationships.

4   The best way to get political allegiance of this generation is connecting them through relationships.

Why are relationships so important to Millennials? We saw three possible answers to this question in the course of our interviews.

First, Millennials learned the importance of relationships, particularly family relationships, from their families. Their parents connected with them to the point of becoming overbearing at times. These helicopter moms and dads communicated loudly through their actions that relationships are important.

Second, Millennials view the world as a much smaller place than predecessor generations. They came into this world with twenty-four-hour news coverage. They have a plethora of social media sites where they can interact with others. They are more likely to take an international trip than any predecessor generation. The Internet gives them an instant view of any part of the globe they desire. By the way, Thom went on the Internet in 1994, when he was thirty-nine years old. Jess was only nine years old. The Internet is still a phenomenon to the Boomers. For the Millennials it's an everyday part of life.

Third, and related to the second, Millennials have the means to stay connected. They have the Internet. They have powerful computers. They have smart phones. And they understand the growing power of cloud computing to connect in ways that were the world of science fiction just a few decades earlier.

Susannah was born in 1987 in Riverside, California. Her mother still lives in Riverside, but her father lives in Colorado Springs with his second wife. She recently graduated from college, and most of her close college and high school friends are scattered all over the United States, and two live in other countries.

The reason we mentioned the diverse locations of her family and friends is her comment that she still stays in touch with most of her friends from high school and college: "I guess most of my friends and I keep up with one another by Facebook, but I text my closest friends a lot. Not too long ago my best friend in college flew to see me. We hadn't seen each other for nearly two years, but it was like we hadn't been apart for any time. We picked up right where we left off."

Susannah represents the Millennial Generation well in her desire to stay connected with others. Indeed, this one motivating factor dominated many of our conversations with those in our studies. If an employer, service organization, religious body, or any other group wants to get the best out of members of this generation, they can't overlook their strong desire to stay connected with others.

Of course, the desire to stay connected to family members is even stronger. As we noted in chapter 3, the Millennials are a family-focused generation. In our study family was the single greatest motivating factor in this generation.

Thom recently asked a room of about a dozen adult Millennials to make a hypothetical choice. They all work for the company where Thom is president. If you could choose between a 10 percent pay raise and two extra days vacation, he asked, what would you choose? The answer was unanimous. All of them would take the extra days vacation. They would, of course, take the extra time to see family and friends.

This generation is truly a relationship generation. If anyone fails to grasp that reality, they have failed to understand the Millennials.

Cap and Gown and Careers

As a reminder, our study included only eighteen- to twenty-nine-year-olds, so we understand that education and careers were issues at the forefront of many Millennials. Indeed, education was the third most important factor in the lives of these young adults, with 17 percent naming education as a high priority in their lives. Careers were close in high importance, named by 16 percent of our Millennial respondents. A few points should be noted here.

First, there is inextricable relationship between education and careers. There is no surprise at this observation. Millennials as a whole are not impressed with degrees and letters after a name. They are, however, interested in advancing their careers, not unlike earlier generations. Of the Millennials we interviewed, who were eighteen- to twenty-nine-years old at the time of our study, 32 percent had already received a college degree. By the time all of these Millennials reach twenty-five years old, nearly four out of ten will likely have a college degree. Of the current U.S. population over twenty-five years old, only 24 percent have a college degree. The Millennials are on a pace to have significantly more college graduates than the rest of the nation as a whole.

Many of them are unequivocal about their desire to get further education. As a rule they realize college graduates have better career paths than those who don't. In this sense the Millennials are aware and pragmatic.

But a second point worth noting is the motivation behind education and career paths. Millennials *do* want to make more money. They are neither nonmaterialistic nor socialistic. We will examine that issue shortly. But, for many of them, their motivation for more education, better careers, and better pay is directly connected to their most significant motivators: family and friends.

"I went straight to grad school after I got my college degree," Debbie told us. She is a twenty-four-year-old MBA student from the Chicago area. "I really don't care much about the prestige of an MBA. That's no big deal to me. What I want is the kind of job where I can have a decent living that will give me some flexibility. I really want to have the time and means to travel and visit my family. I may be unrealistic, but

I don't want to wait ten to twenty years before I'm in a good financial position with a good job."

Of course, at least half of the Millennials will not get a college degree. Some will start college and never finish. Others will never begin at all. But, with few exceptions in our interviews, this group of young adults is driven to have some type of good career that will give the means to stay connected with family and friends. Money is not unimportant to this generation. Indeed, in light of some of the noble goals of the Millennials we have mentioned, it might be surprising to hear some of their attitudes about money.

 ## Show Me the Money?

Are the Millennials driven by money? After listening to this group of young adults for hundreds of hours, we concluded that, as a whole, they *are not* driven by money. Still, we must also say that income levels and money *are* important to them.

Perhaps there is some confusion with our assessment. The accumulation of money is not a goal for the Millennials. They do not, as a whole, view income levels as matters of prestige and pride. They do, however, have a utilitarian perspective of money. Stated simply, they see money as a vehicle to do what they want to do and to have what they desire.

For that reason we can now understand why 83 percent of the Millennials said that having a high income was important to them. But, if we dissect that number into two components, we see that only 34 percent strongly agree, while 49 percent agree somewhat. These numbers better reflect the caution Millennials place when they say money is important to them.

"My parents have always been materialistic," said Kennedy, a twenty-eight-year-old medical intern from Fort Worth, Texas. "I love them, but they've always been the classic 'keep up with the Jones' family. Sometimes it was funny, but other times it got pretty pathetic."

But Kennedy was one of the 83 percent of Millennials who said that having a high income was important. "I had to answer that question honestly," he began, "but I know I'm light-years different from my parents. Mom and Dad bought stuff just to keep a level of prestige. They are prideful in their material stuff. They used to drive a seven series BMW, and now they drive the top of the line Lexus. It's all about the prestige for them."

So, we asked Kennedy, how is your desire for high income different from your parents? "I want to have a good income to travel, to see family and friends, and to have enough money to give to causes I believe in," he responded. "I'm not really into buying things. Okay, maybe I do have a weakness for anything Apple. But it's nothing like my parents."

While the Millennials may be a bit nobler in their stated reasons for desiring high income and wealth, the bottom line is that they still have money as a motivating force in their lives. And it's not all about the good cash flow that a high income brings. They are also motivated to accumulate wealth.

Coincidently, the number of Millennials who are motivated to have a high income, 83 percent, is the same number who are motivated to become wealthy. The division between the "agree strongly" and the "agree somewhat" is a bit different though. Those who feel more strongly about wealth accounted for 40 percent of the total, while those who agree somewhat were close at 43 percent.

The point is still inescapable. Millennials see money as a major motivating force in their lives. They may assign noble motives to their desires for income and wealth, but money is still a huge issue for them. At least in this regard, they are not that much different from their Boomer parents.

③ Religion as a Motivating Force

Religious institutions have failed to be a force in the lives of the Millennials. Perhaps one of the most surprising aspects of our research was how little this generation values religion of any kind. They are not antagonistic against religions and religious people; they simply see them as unimportant and irrelevant. In chapter 10 we will unpack this issue in greater detail. For now we can state with much certitude that the Millennials are largely a nonreligious generation.

Overall spiritual matters were unimportant to these young adults. Only 13 percent of them viewed religion and spiritual matters with any degree of importance. What is shocking is to see how certain subgroups responded. For example, among the Millennials who are self-described Christians, only 18 percent said their religion was important to them. Among those who held to basic Christian doctrine (the majority of self-described Christians do not), only 38 percent said their faith was important.

There was only one group in our study where a majority said their faith was important to them. We called them "Evangelicals" because they held to all of the major historic and biblical doctrines of the Christian faith, including the total veracity of the Bible. In that group 65 percent said their faith was important to them. But that number can't be verified in our study with statistical accuracy since only 6 percent of Millennials could be described as Evangelicals.

In chapter 10 we will introduce you to some of the Millennials who have written off religion in their lives. Kayleigh provides a preview of that mind-set for now. She was born in upstate New York but now resides in Colorado. When we asked her questions about religion, her response was typical of her generation. "Religion?" she questioned. "Honestly, I just don't think that much about religion. I guess it's just not on my radar screen. I guess I have too many other priorities in my life. I'm not anti-religious, and I'm not mad at churches or religious people. It's their thing and that's fine. It's just not my thing."

For those who may have been hopeful that the Millennials would be a more religious or Christian generation, the results of our interviews will prove sorely disappointing. Overall their religious faith does not motivate them. In fact, most of them don't have a religious faith to motivate them. Like Kayleigh, most Millennials assert that religion is just not their thing.

Looking to the Government?

In 2008 the people of the United States elected the first African-American president in history. Democrat Barack Obama defeated Republican John McCain soundly by a 53 percent to 46 percent margin. The electoral votes were even more lopsided in Obama's favor, 365 to 173.

When the postelection discussion began to unfold, much of the voting analyses met expectations. But one group had received only modest attention going into the election. While it was generally conceded that young adults were largely in favor of Obama, there was uncertainty if this group would actually turn out on election day.

Keep in mind that in 2008 the oldest Millennial was twenty-eight years old; and the youngest was only eight years old. Only about one-half of this generation was actually eligible to vote. But the response of this generation that did vote was astounding.

The Millennials voted for Barack Obama by an overwhelming 66 to 32 percent margin. Most exit polls showed that this generation strongly favored gay marriage. Similar polls revealed that the young adults opposed the war in Iraq; some of the polls indicated that this number was as high as eight out of ten.

This young generation was also clear on their expectations of the federal government. They wanted more centralized power in the government, and they thought Obama would more likely deliver on that expectation. Different exit polls generally demonstrated that eight out of ten wanted a stronger governmental role in our lives.

For example, on the issue of universal health care, Millennials by a 71 percent to 29 percent margin thought the federal government should guarantee health-care coverage for all Americans.

At least in 2008 the Millennials proved to be a generation motivated by a strong centralized federal government. And our study of the Millennials indicates that the same desire is still alive and well today.

What has prompted this generation to see government as the solution to many of the social problems, as well as the answer to some of their own personal needs? First, we must have an awareness of key issues that surrounded both the 2008 election and the timing of our study. During those years the United States was experiencing the worst economic downturn since the Great Depression. Unemployment was high, and most other economic indicators were dismal as well.

It is not unusual to see people look to the government for solutions when few alternatives seem available. What will be interesting to monitor is the attitude of the Millennials toward government as the economy improves and as they become older. Will they shift from their current strong government leanings? Or have they been so marked by the severity of the recession and the failure of other institutions that this generation will remain a big-government generation?

The latter question brings up another possible explanation. The desire for big government could be a matter of default. No other organizations have stepped up significantly, so the government is the only logical place for solutions.

A number of the Millennials did blame two institutions specifically: the family and the church. Rob of Tulsa, Oklahoma, summed up the matter of both institutions succinctly. "Look, I wish we didn't always have to look to the government for solutions and help," he stated. "But where are we to look? The American family is in terrible shape, and churches are too busy fighting among themselves to make any difference. Is there any other place to turn?"

More than six out of ten Millennials felt that the government should be responsible for providing their retirement. Even though the number represents a significant majority, the sense of entitlement was not strong. Only 20 percent had a strong opinion that this was a proper role of government.

The results were similar on government-provided health care. Two-thirds of the respondents told us that it was the government's responsibility to provide everyone adequate health-care coverage. But on this issue only 26 percent felt strongly about it. Many of the Millennials seem to be seeking an expanded role of government, but they are doing so reluctantly. They have turned to a more centralized government because they know of no other alternatives.

(5) "I Believe in Me"

Millennials are incredibly motivated to make a difference in this world. And they are likely to do so. If you don't believe it, just ask one of them.

Nicole was born in 1984. Her parents divorced when she was eleven, and she still recalls the pain of the breakup today. Like many children of broken homes, one of the biggest issues for her was seeing both parents remarry. She lived with her mother and stepfather in Missouri, but she visited her father and stepmother regularly in south Florida.

"It was a bummer," she recalls. "I never could have a normal summer or normal holidays like other kids. My little brother and I were sent back and forth. It got really old."

So we asked Nicole if she has negative feelings about her parents today in light of the pain and hassle the divorce brought to her life. Her emphatic response surprised us, "Absolutely not!" she said with strong measure. "I love both of my parents. Yeah, it hurt when they got a divorce, but they are still my best friends. They've always been there for me and always believed in me."

They've always believed in me. We heard those or similar words from countless Millennials. To be sure, not all the Millennials had positive role models for parents, and not all had healthy relationships. But as we noted in chapter 3, a large number of the members of this generation were told by their parents that they could do anything they put their mind to do.

They believed it then. And they still believe it today.

We asked Millennials to respond to a simple statement: "I believe I can do something great." If you think the Millennials may doubt themselves, think again. Those who agreed with that statement represented 96 percent of those we surveyed! And when we analyze the responses on the Likert scale, the level of confidence among these young adults is even more evident.

Sixty percent strongly agreed with the statement; and 36 percent agreed somewhat. Of the negative responses, 4 percent disagreed somewhat; and absolutely *none* of the twelve hundred respondents disagreed strongly. This generation is one confident group of people.

Ashley is typical of the Millennials in her belief in herself. "I really see the sky as the limit for what I can do in this world," she said without a hint of modesty. "I guess some people think that being president of the United States or CEO of a big company is a superambitious goal. Not me. That's not how I think. I don't think in terms of positions or money; I really think about doing something to change the world for the better. You know, I really believe I can do something like that. I really believe in me."

Potential employers and others who meet these self-confident Millennials may be turned off a bit by their brashness and self-focus. But there is a more positive aspect to consider. Sure, they have tons of self-confidence that borders on arrogance. But that belief in self can be channeled into highly productive work. If Millennials can just be a little patient and willing to pay the price in some areas, they may indeed be the next great generation. They believe in themselves. Maybe others should believe in them as well.

The good news is that this self-confidence may well translate into meaningful contributions to society. Our research tells us that the Millennials, in addition to believing they will make a difference, also desire to make a difference for the good of the world. We made a simple statement to get their responses: "I am motivated to serve others in society." Amazingly 77 percent of this generation affirmed the statement.

In our interview with Ashley, noted above, she said that she thought she could change the world for the better. Aaron, born in 1983 like Ashley, also is motivated with altruistic motives. "I think my generation is not really impressed with the rock stars of our parents' generation," he began. "We've seen the sleazy side of politics, so politicians don't impress us. We've seen the total lack of ethics of some CEOs, so they don't impress us. And we've seen the moral failure of clergy so they don't impress us either."

Aaron continued, "Most people I know in my generation could care less about titles and prestige. We just want to do something that makes a difference. I really believe my generation will be the generation that turns this messed up country and world around."

As we noted, the Millennials are not lacking in confidence.

To their credit, this generation does not think they have arrived. Indeed, another moniker that might fit the Millennials is "the learning generation." When we asked them to respond to the statement, "I have a great appetite for learning," the results were impressive. An overwhelming 95 percent of the Millennials answered the question positively, and six out of ten responded with a strong affirmation.

This generation is motivated by learning opportunities. Such is the reason they will become America's most educated generations. But their hunger for learning is not limited to formal settings. Many of them told us they were voracious readers. And they overwhelming expressed their desire to learn from others in one-on-one settings. More on that shortly.

Indeed, if we are to see the best of this generation, we must tap into their strong desires to make a difference and to make a major contribution to society. Even now, some of the Millennials are wondering if older generations will allow them to fulfill their potential. At the point of our survey, 85 percent of these young adults felt they have a lot of unused potential, and 42 percent felt strongly about this perceived state.

"I have a lot of drive and ambition," Lisa told us. She was twenty-four years old at the time of our interview. "I hope I don't get too frustrated or cynical though. But it seems like those older than my generation may not give us the opportunities we want and need. I really want to make a difference. I hope I'm given the opportunity."

The respondents were split on whether the Baby Boomers would truly give them the opportunities where they can make a difference. Indeed it was almost a fifty/fifty split among those who responded "agree" or "disagree" with this statement: "Baby Boomers who know me still tend to doubt my abilities because of my generation."

Those born before the Baby Boomers are sometimes called "the greatest generation." They believed they could make a difference, and they seized the opportunities afforded them. Will the Millennials be the next "greatest generation"? Or will they grow cynical and frustrated because they have been denied the opportunities to make a difference?

Where Do They Turn?

They believe in themselves. They believe they can make a difference. They state emphatically that they will make a contribution to society. But they also said they don't have all the answers. They are hungry to learn. They will get the education. They will be self-learners. But they are also motivated to learn from others. Where then do they turn?

In light of our earlier discussions, it should come as no surprise that the Millennials turned to their parents for one of their primary sources of influence. An amazingly high 88 percent indicated that their parents were a source of influence. A majority, 51 percent, said that parents were strong influences on them. It is expected, then, that the Millennials turned to their mothers and fathers for advice and guidance. Again, the number is high: 85 percent turn to their parents for advice.

"My parents have been my champions all of my life," said Stephanie, born in 1989. "It's only natural for me to call on them when I need help or advice. They live in the Boston area, and I live across the country in Oregon. But that doesn't matter. We talk to each other every week, sometimes several days a week. If I have a question on almost anything, I call Mom or Dad."

The Millennials are truly a family friendly generation. Those who are married said that their spouse is the number one influence in their lives. Again the numbers were nothing short of remarkable. Among the married Millennials 96 percent said their spouse was a source of positive influence. Three percent indicated the spouse was no influence, and only 1 percent said that the influence was negative. It would seem that the Millennials are getting a healthy start on their marriages.

Jeremy was unwavering in his response. "That's easy," he said, "I turn to Donna [his wife]. She was my best friend before we got married, so there's no reason why she shouldn't be my best friend today. And you should always turn to your best friend for help and advice."

Jeremy is not alone in his sentiments. Ninety-three percent of the married Millennials said they turn to their spouse "a lot" or "some." Only 7 percent responded "very little" or "none."

The centrality of the family for advice and guidance became apparent beyond parents and spouses. More than two-thirds of the Millennials turn to extended family members such as siblings or grandparents.

This generation is truly open to guidance in a myriad of relationships. For example, 81 percent of the Millennials indicated that friends were positive influences in their lives.

We could go on with a plethora of statistics, but we are to the point of redundancy. Millennials believe they can make a difference. They are not so arrogant to think they have all the answers. Indeed they are open to learning from a variety of sources, both formal and informal. It will be interesting to see if older generations embrace their noble ambitions. If not, there may not be a next "greatest generation."

The Future Just Arrived

The clichés are abundant. "Time flies." "Where did all the years go?" "They grow up so fast." "It seems like yesterday they were little."

The clichés are abundant for a reason. They're true.

It does seem like yesterday that my (Thom's) three sons were little boys. Time has flown. They did grow up fast.

My sons, born in 1980, 1982, and 1985, are all Millennials. Now they are all grown men. They have wives. They have children. They have entered the workforce. And each of them, in his own way, is trying to make a difference.

I just blinked my eyes and the future arrived.

I am not a spokesman for my generation; so many Baby Boomers may disagree with me. But my perspective is that we are leaving our children a world that is in a much sadder state than when the baton was passed to us. May I speak directly to the Millennials for a few moments?

We have borrowed from your future and left you an incomprehensible national debt. We have polluted the world and left you dirtier air and water. Our politicians have failed you. Our religious leaders have failed you. Our business leaders have failed you. It is no wonder that you care little for the institutions of our nation. It is no wonder that you have always had a cynical view of those institutions.

We have created such a system of entitlements that everyone seems to be asking for their next handout. But we have not adequately funded those entitlements so we borrowed a bit more from your future.

We have left you wars. And it seems like we are engaged in the new habit of fighting multiple wars at the same time. We have left you in the fear of terrorism. I know you can't blame the Baby Boomers for terrorists, but those terrorists have taken advantage of the weaker nation we left you.

It seems as though the one significant gift we left you was our belief in you. I know sometimes you were our trophy children, and we pushed you to accomplish things for our own egos. But most of the time we truly did want the best for you. We really do love you. And we really do believe that you can make a difference.

It won't be easy to reverse the problems we have created, but you can do it. You have the desire. You have the abilities. You have the education, both formal and informal. Yes, you can do it.

Then perhaps, in thirty or forty years, when you pass the baton of leadership to your children in the next generation, you will give them a better place than we left you. If nothing else, we leave you with our confidence that you, the Millennials, will become the next great generation.

A Place to Begin

As the new millennium dawned in 2000, something significant other than the turning of the calendar was taking place. In that year the Millennials began to enter the workforce. Most employers were unprepared for them. Some were irritated by them, and others delighted in them.

The moment was significant. The leading edge of seventy-eight million people entered into places where they would make their livelihood. And they entered with high hopes, unusual expectations, and significant ambitions. Most of them entered the workplaces with a simple desire: They want to change the world.

This arena of opportunity is the first test for the hopes, dreams, and motivations of America's largest generation. By 2025 most of them will have made their entry. How are they being received? Are their motivations being used, or are their dreams being crushed? Are they really on the path to change the world, or have they given up already and discovered the negative forces of cynicism?

It is thus vitally important for us to find out what is taking place with the Millennials and what will take place in those areas where they are first employed. We begin that important discussion in the next chapter.

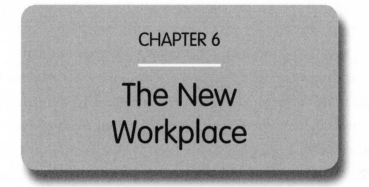

CHAPTER 6

The New Workplace

The meeting was not exactly what I (Thom) expected. A dozen or so twenty-something employees met with me in a conference room. There was really no agenda for the meeting. I was hoping to get to know better some of the young employees at the organization where I serve as president. With nearly five thousand employees, the company is rather large, and, thus, relationships are difficult to develop with most who work there.

Of course, I did not expect the one-hour meeting to engender close relationships. I did hope, however, to listen carefully to this representative group of Millennials at my company. I assumed they would be engaging.

I was not disappointed.

The energy level was palpable the moment I entered the conference room. Now I realize that their youthfulness contributed significantly to the energy. And I also realize that they were excited to have this meeting with the president of the company. But there was more to it than those two factors.

These Millennials at my company are different from other workers I have known at several different places of employment. Most of the differences are good; some are a bit challenging.

Immediately these young adults wanted to show me some of their most recent work. Most in the room were in creative media, and some of the promos and movies they developed were nothing short of incredible. They told me about how they had accomplished the work on a shoestring budget. I was blown away.

I had heard that a number of Millennials at my company wanted our dress code changed. And I guess if they had written the dress code, it wouldn't look like it does in its present state. Tucked in shirttails and prohibition of facial jewelry on males probably is a bit archaic to them. But I was surprised that the issue was not primary.

These Millennials wanted to talk to me about working at a place that makes a difference. They wanted to affirm that they were a part of an organization that makes a contribution to society. And, more than anything else, they wanted an employer that encourages a healthy work/life balance and respects their desires to give priority to family and friends.

I really did respect their priorities.

I sensed some challenges as well. For example, I detected impatience with job progress and responsibilities. I guess I could have been a bit old-fashioned and concluded that they really didn't want to pay the price to get ahead and to earn added responsibilities. And I could have taken their confidence to be a bit overboard and desired to see a bit more humility.

Still, I could have read them wrongly. Perhaps I needed to see their ambition a bit more positively. Perhaps I needed to view their confidence with great expectations that they would soon be making major contributions.

The net effect of the meeting for me, though, was positive. I walked away from the meeting excited that we had such enthusiastic Millennials at our workplace.

The research we conducted confirmed much of what took place in the meeting. The Millennials are entering the workplace by storm. Baby Boomers are retiring by the millions each year. And these young adults, at least at the entry level, are filling most of the vacancies.

As the president of a fairly large company, I am intensely interested in this generation. After meeting with many Millennials in this study and beyond, I can now say I am fascinated by this generation in the workforce. But I fear many employers are not ready for them. Though their entry can be an energetic addition to the workforce, they are different from previous generations. That reality can be a bit unsettling.

The Millennials Are Coming to a Workplace Near You

Every generation is different, and thus every employer has a learning curve as young employees enter the workforce.

Most of the Millennials have a positive and unique relationship with their parents. In chapter 3 we looked in detail at the importance of family to this generation. These positive relationships are major factors in the workplace. For example, the Millennials tend to relate well to people in older generations. This respect and relational tie will be important in the workplace.

Second, as we have seen throughout this book, the Millennials as a whole are not lacking in confidence. Their parents told them they could accomplish anything. They bring that same confidence into the workplace. Some employers will see their attitude as lacking in humility. Other employers will view the Millennials' self-confidence as an opportunity to strengthen the organization.

They started entering the workforce in 2000, and they will continue to come until sometime around 2025. Then there will be as many as seventy-eight million of them in places of employment. They are coming whether we are ready or not. And they are coming in the largest numbers ever.

✳ The Ambitious Generation

Throughout this book we have labeled the Millennials with different monikers. Another name that could be given to them is "the Ambitious Generation." This group of young adults desires to succeed. They want to know that career success is possible in their places of employment. And they will likely keep moving until they find the place that provides them a clear career ladder.

Trisha got her master's degree before she took a job out of college. She completed some internships that gave her some experience, but she is now in her first full-time employment.

"I like my work," she told us without equivocation. "I was fortunate to get a job in my field in the middle of the recession. So far the experience has been positive, and my coworkers are great."

With such a glowing report we assumed that Trisha had a long-term view of her tenure at this job. She corrected us quickly. "That's not necessarily the case. I like many aspects of my job, but I've been here eighteen months, and I'm not so sure my future is good here."

We were curious so we asked her to elaborate about her tenuous future at the company. "I've seen a lot a people here stuck in the same job for years," she began. "Some of the folks who've hit dead ends seem to be great people. I can't understand why they haven't been given other opportunities. If I can't move ahead in this job, then I will move on elsewhere."

Many in the Millennial Generation have been told that there are no limits to what they can accomplish. Many of the "helicopter parents" reinforced that belief. So when these young adults find jobs they perceive have little upward mobility, they will likely leave at the first possibility.

The numbers in our research are staggering. Over 84 percent of the Millennials told us that career success is important to them. It seems that some employers with whom we've spoken perceive that Millennials do not care much about climbing the ladder at work. Nothing could be further from the truth. This is an ambitious generation indeed. Their expectations for themselves and their career success are high.

Some employers did not notice this restlessness among the Millennial workers during the Great Recession. The bad economy temporarily masked low retention rates. But as the economy improves and more jobs become available, watch for Millennials to move quickly from one job opportunity to another. Employers will be challenged to retain this ambitious group of young adults. If they can't move upward, many will move onward.

What Attracts Millennials to the Workplace?

Our study of the Millennials made us look at the workplace with different perspectives. Business as usual will neither attract nor retain these young adults. Rob is a twenty-seven-year-old accountant in a midsize firm. He shared with us how his generation is different from the other people where he works.

"I try not to be a whiner," Rob began. "I don't want to get a reputation at work for acting like a know-it-all, especially since I'm one of the young guys. But I will tell you that I really get frustrated with some of my coworkers who are older than me. They seem to be so political and try to cover their butts all the time. Most of them seem to be only concerned about protecting their jobs. When I work with them, we sometimes can't make any progress because they won't challenge the status quo. Not me. There's more to life than this job."

That "more to life than this job" attitude first defines the Millennials in the workplace. Indeed, it is the first of what we called "the big five" in job selection and retention for this generation.

The Big Five Factors in Job Selection

Five factors played critically important roles in job selection and satisfaction with the Millennials. Each of these areas was selected by at least eight out of ten of those we surveyed. We begin with the issue that reflected that there is "more to life than this job."

Factor 1: Work/life balance. They love and respect their families. They have close relationships with their parents. Those who are married give their marriages high priority. Those who have children are typically devoted to them. And they value good friendships. Relationships are key to this generation.

It is then no surprise that work/life balance is vitally important to the Millennials in their job selection and in their decision to remain at their present place of employment. We asked those we surveyed to list factors that were important in selecting a job. Their responses were not mutually exclusive, so the total is far more than 100 percent.

The Millennials in our study responded to ten different issues in selecting a job. There was a clear statistical break in their responses from the first five to the last five. We were particularly interested to see the factors where the Millennials responded "extremely important." For example, slightly more than half, 51 percent, named work/life balance as an extremely important factor in selecting a job. This response was the only one where more than half responded so strongly.

Several factors likely engendered this response. Of course relationships with families and friends were foremost among the offered explanations. If a job does not allow the Millennial to have time to spend with family and friends, he or she is likely to be dissatisfied with the work environment. That issue is indeed paramount in their job selection.

But there seems to be another looming issue behind this response. In some of the open-end responses, we heard Millennials talk about the brevity of life and the uncertainty of life. Most of them did not speak in these terms with a fatalistic attitude as much as they did with a healthy dose of reality.

Keep in mind the ages of those we surveyed. They are the older Millennials with birth years between 1980 and 1991. Their ages ranged from ten to twenty-one on September 11, 2001. They were profoundly affected by the terrorist attacks in the United States on that fatal day. Their world changed in seconds.

They could no longer view the world through a lens of safety and security as they had to this point. They realized that life was fragile and uncertain. Many of the Millennials can't see themselves in jobs that hinder them from focusing on what really matters.

Though not all of those we surveyed stated the issue explicitly, it would seem that Noel, born in 1982, expressed the feelings of many in his generation.

"I think 9-11 will be the shaping event of our generation. It sure was for me," he told us. "I have replayed the events of that day a thousand times in my mind. It really makes me focus on things that matter most, like family and friends. When I looked for a job, one of the most important criteria for me was that I would have to have a meaningful life outside my work. Life is just too short and uncertain to spend too many days doing nothing but work, eat, and sleep."

The challenge for employers with this generation is providing an environment that values the balanced life while encouraging Millennials to be diligent workers as well. Indeed some Millennials complain that some in their generation take the work/life balance to an extreme.

Sandra was one of those who saw some of her peers not performing well in her company because they neglected work too often for other issues. "I have a coworker who was born the same year I was, 1984. He so neglected his work for family and other matters that he didn't get his job done. He was warned on several occasions, but he kind of proudly said that his family, friends, and health came first."

She paused for a moment, but we anticipated her next sentence. "He really was surprised when he got fired last month," she said bluntly. "But no one who worked with him was surprised."

Work/life balance is a challenge for both employers and Millennial employees. But the Millennials themselves gave us some insights on dealing with this matter. We will address possible solutions at the end of this chapter.

Factor 2: "Show me the money." As we noted earlier, there seems to be this strange misperception with some that money is not that important to Millennials. In chapter 9 we will delve into that matter deeply. For now, we simply state unequivocally: money is important to Millennials.

They may be different in many ways from previous generations, but they are not completely different. Income is a big factor in both job selection and retention. It was the second most important factor in job selection, noted by 49 percent of the respondents as extremely important. Nine out of ten said that money was an important factor at some level of importance. In fact, the difference between the first factor, work/life balance, and the second factor, compensation, is not statistically significant.

Millennials seem to have less interest in material items than the desire for flexibility and connecting socially. Those two issues explain why many of them strongly desire a job with good compensation. Jeff is typical of this group in his responses to us.

"It's kind of funny," he began. "My parents are Baby Boomers, and they are about as materialistic as you can be. They love their cars, their home, and their boat. I've seen them buy things just because someone else has it. When I mention that to them, they tell me it's not so. But I know it is."

Jeff paused for a moment with a big grin on his face. "Now I find myself wanting a good income too. I always said I really wouldn't care too much how much I got paid, but I was wrong. The big difference I see, though, is how we spend our money."

We asked Jeff to expand on his last statement. "My parents spend money on things, you know, toys," he began. "But I use my money for smart phones and good computers so I can stay in touch with family and friends. And I like to travel, too, to see my family. I really like having a good income to stay connected to people that I'm close to."

Though our research has no empirical data to compare the Millennials' attitude toward money with earlier generations, we do get the impression that this young adult group knows more about money at this point in their lives than their older counterparts. Such an assumption would seem commonsensical. This is the generation that has had their parents hovering over them from birth. Many of them, as we will see in chapter 9, learned valuable lessons about finances from their parents. They thus likely have a better understanding of compensation issues early in their careers.

Further, this generation has access to a seemingly unlimited number of sources via the Internet that provide all sorts of information about job compensation. Many of these young adults thus come well prepared to negotiate salary and benefits. They likewise know when their current jobs aren't meeting their expectations financially since they have timely market data.

We have spoken with many employers who are surprised that compensation is such a major issue for the Millennials. They have heard that this generation is more concerned about family or friends or making the world better than how much money they make. The Millennials may have different reasons why money is such an important issue to them in the job market than earlier generations. But the research clearly reveals that employers and potential employees better prepare for a generation that will demand that you "show me the money."

Factor 3: Millennials just want to have fun. They have played with electronic games for as far back as they can remember. They have been to unbelievably sophisticated and technologically advanced amusement parks. They have watched movies on screens that bring the image incredibly close to life. Most of them can't remember not having a computer. And those computers not only served as educational tools; they entertained this generation as well.

This generation knows how to have fun.

Indeed this generation insists on having fun.

Employers need to be prepared. Some companies are still acting like all their employees were born before 1946. The culture is one of sobriety, low-key conversations, and humorless leadership. Then there is the culture shock when a Millennial invades the organization and declares that it's party time.

When Millennials have a choice between jobs, they will likely take the one they perceive to be fun. They know that even IBM shed its blue suits and white shirts years ago. For this generation serious work and a fun environment are not mutually exclusive. Nearly nine out of ten Millennials told us that the ability to have fun on the job was a significant factor in choosing a job or staying with a current employer. Amazingly, 41 percent of this generation said that fun on the job was "extremely important" to them. This high priority was only exceeded by work/life balance and good compensation.

Kevin was one of the Millennials who advocated fun on the job. He is a twenty-nine-year-old engineer working in a midsize firm in Tacoma, Washington. There was no equivocation in his voice about his choice to work there. "I guess I was fortunate," he told us. "I went into a field where the job demand was still good. I had my choice of four jobs. The pay was comparable in all four, so I took the job where the employees seemed to have the most fun. In fact, when I interviewed with several employees, that was the theme I heard over and over. Everybody just seemed happy, and after a year I still think I made a great decision. I actually enjoy getting up each morning to go to work."

Throughout our interviews we heard the "life is too short not to have fun" theme. In many different parts of our study, we again noted that this 9-11 generation really does have a grasp on the brevity of life. Many of them also told us that their Boomer parents influenced them to have fun. "Mom and Dad still sometimes act like they're in the 1960s," noted Lilly, a Millennial from Colorado Springs. "They embarrassed me a lot when I was a teenager, but now I really enjoy them. They showed me how to have fun."

Employers need to be ready for the fun generation. The Millennials' dream jobs are at places like Google, Qualcomm, and SAS. Though the pay and the financial benefits are excellent, the more common accolades are that they are "cool jobs" and "fun jobs." Fun jobs are in for the Millennials.

Factor 4: Flexibility is almost as important as money. More than eight of ten Millennials desire jobs that have some level of flexibility in their schedules. And almost four out of ten ranked the factor as "extremely important" in selecting a job.

Based on our earlier discussions, this factor makes good sense. This generation is the family generation. They strongly desire the time and flexibility to be able to visit family and friends and to take family vacations. Most of them don't hesitate to work long and hard, but they would like to be rewarded with a flexible schedule.

Most of the Millennials desire some flexibility, but they realize employers can't change everything to accommodate them. Noted Pam from Atlanta: "I'm not looking for flexible hours every week. I just want to be able to take two or three long weekends a year without giving up vacation time. I more than make up any hours that I might miss. I'm a hard worker, and I really just want some modest flexibility.

Pam is not getting that flexibility in her current employment, so she is looking for another job. "The economy hasn't helped my job mobility," she explained, "but it won't be like this forever. I'll be able to find a better job in the near future."

Keep in mind the first four "extremely important" factors for the Millennials in job selection: work/life balance, compensation, fun in the job, and flexible hours. A common thread runs through each of these factors. The thread is relationships.

Millennials desire work/life balance to keep healthy relationships with family and friends. They look for good compensation so they will have the resources to connect with family
and friends. They want fun on the job because they know that
fun times help build relationships. And they seek flexible hours
so they can have the time to see those people who are close to
them.

It's all about relationships. The employer who can grasp that
reality and respond to it well will be the employer that has a
motivated and productive group of Millennial employees.

Factor 5: But they do want structure and feedback.
The Millennials' desire for flexibility and their equal desire for
structure are not mutually exclusive. We noted in the previous
section that relationships drive the desire for flexibility. The
relational world of Millennials also ties with their desire for
structure and feedback.

Many Millennials told us of their positive relationships with
adults as they were growing up. Foremost among the adults
with whom they have such good relationships are their parents.
Mom and Dad were often there to encourage their children to
get the good grade, to excel in the sport, or to do the dance with
excellence. The Millennials are accustomed to a structured life
with a lot of feedback.

Since many in this generation have positive relationships
with their parents, they were able to develop similar relationships with teachers, coaches, and instructors. Again they found
themselves in a structured environment where they were receiving regular feedback.

I (Thom) see that same propensity in my three adult sons. To this day I get regular calls, e-mails, and texts seeking feedback and advice on academic work, job-related matters, and personal finances, to name a few. Sam, Art, and Jess aren't hesitant to seek input, and they even handle my constructive criticism well.

Most Millennials will not function well vocationally if they aren't getting regular feedback. They told us on multiple occasions that the feedback needs to be both informal and formal. They don't mind the traditional annual review, but they desire more. They are accustomed to an ongoing dialogue with someone about their performance and expectations of them.

The challenge is that Millennial employees will need more attention than most other employees get or need. In fact, in one of our survey questions, three-fourths of this generation told us that they want to be mentored by a leader. The good news is that they respond well to the input given them, including comments and suggestions of constructive criticism.

Four Surprises in Job Selection

Prior to our research interviewing twelve hundred Millennials, we both had some preconceived notions about this generation, particularly in the area of job selection. On four of the factors we raised with these young adults, we were truly surprised. Our hypothesis was that each of these would be extremely important to the Millennial employee. Such was not the case.

As a point of clarification, we do not want to suggest that these factors were unimportant to the Millennial employee. The surprise rather was that they didn't view these issues to be those of highest importance.

Surprise 1: Contribution to society. While a majority of the Millennials do prefer to work at an organization that makes a contribution to society, only a small portion of this generation said that it was an extremely important factor. Only 18 percent rated this issue as one of high importance.

We were surprised at this low number, and we were perplexed with the reasons it was so low. In numerous conversations with Millennials, few were willing to say that it was unimportant. The best we could discern from their responses was that other issues overshadowed it.

For example, Robert of Nebraska summed others' sentiments well. "Who doesn't want to work for a company that's making the world a better place to live?" he asked rhetorically. "I mean, you sure won't catch me working for a tobacco company or some other obvious threat to society. But that's just not the major issue I think about when looking for a job. I want a job that pays well and gives me some freedom. Everything else is secondary to me."

Thus the only conclusion we could derive was that other matters were of greater importance. Having a job at a company that makes a contribution to society is nice for the Millennials; it's just not the most important thing.

Surprise 2: Casual dress. Earlier I (Thom) referred to a meeting I had with a group of young adult leaders at the company where I serve as president. Though I really didn't plan, nor did I know, the direction of the meeting, I had a good idea what one of their issues would be. After listening to them share what they did for the company, I called for a time of open questions. They could ask anything of me they desired, or they could make comments, criticisms, and recommendations.

I waited for it. I knew our dress code of business casual was not the preference of many of these young adults. And I just knew that these Millennials would bombard me with questions and complaints about our dress code. I waited for it.

I was wrong.

There were many issues on the tables and many great questions. I love the first one off the bat: "What is your dream for this company?" But no one mentioned the dress code.

I finally asked them why it wasn't an issue. First, they told me that, while it would be nice if they could wear jeans and tennis shoes, it just wasn't that big of a deal to them. There were more pressing matters. Second, they reminded me that I had explained the dress code to the organization. We often have clients walking in who would be uncomfortable with a very casual dress. We needed to be certain that we didn't create discomfort for guests by what we wore.

They were satisfied with my explanation. They were ready to move on to more important matters. And at least, they reminded me, our company doesn't require our male employees to wear that hanging noose called a tie.

Only half of the Millennials regarded casual attire as even a matter of moderate importance in their jobs. Even more surprising, at least from our initial assumptions, was that only 15 percent assigned high importance to the matter of wearing casual attire. As an interesting aside, the higher the education level, the less important this issue was to the Millennial employee. Among those with high school degrees only, 17 percent regarded dress code as extremely important. That number dropped to 13 percent for college graduates and only 5 percent for those with graduate degrees.

Surprise 3: Environmentally conscious. In the next chapter we will look at the Millennials and the green issue. Just how environmentally radical are they? Our conclusion from those we surveyed was simply that they are green but not as green as many seem to think. We will wait for chapter 7 to unfold that issue more fully.

We can say at this point, with a level of certainty, that the matter of environmental consciousness is an issue in job selection but not a big issue. Only about half of the Millennials saw it as an issue at all. A small number, 12 percent, considered a company's environmental record to be an extremely important matter in their job selection.

Though we did not analyze subgroups sufficiently to offer explanations, we did find some interesting attitudes in these groups. For example, more Asians, 63 percent, placed an emphasis on the environment and job selection than any other group. Hispanics were the most passionate about this issue with 27 percent indicating it was "extremely important" in job selection. Evangelicals assigned the least importance to this issue in job selection, with only 36 percent giving it any level of importance.

Surprise 4: Working from home. Telecommuting, or working from home, is not an issue for most Millennials. Only 11 percent said it was an extremely important issue. To the contrary, the vast majority of the Millennials prefer the structure and accountability that comes with a place of work.

"I have no desire to work from home," said Stephanie, a twenty-eight-year-old from Des Moines, Iowa. "I need the structure and accountability to get my work done. I fear that I would end up surfing the net a lot and goofing off if I stayed at home. And I really want someone to mentor me. It's hard to get that unless you see somebody on a regular basis.

By the way, this matter of mentoring and supervisors came up quite a bit in our conversation. That information gave us even further insight into the Millennials' perspectives on the workplace.

Looking for Leadership

We indicated earlier that three-fourths of the Millennials would like a mentor in their lives. We were thus interested to find out what their experiences were so far in the workplace, particularly in their relationships with their supervisors. Our conclusions are mixed at this point.

For example, eight of ten Millennials indicated that their supervisor understands their work-related needs. But only 28 percent felt strongly about this matter. Noted Maria from San Francisco: "My boss is a good guy. And I know he thinks he does what's best for me at work. But he really doesn't fully understand me. He'll try to lead me with old paradigms, but he's never really made an attempt to get to know me well enough to understand I don't work out of those paradigms. I wish he would sometimes ask me an open-ended question like, 'How can we make this place a better workplace?' I give him a good grade for effort, but he has a long way to go to really understand what I'm looking for at work."

Similarly, three-fourths of the young adults said that they trust their supervisors, but only 27 percent felt strongly in that direction. The feedback was similar to that noted by Maria. Most of the Millennials don't think their supervisor would intentionally do something detrimental to them or to their work. But many are concerned by what their supervisors *don't* know and the potential harm that could be caused by their ignorance.

We did not detect arrogance or attitudes of superiority by most of the Millennials in our study. But we definitely heard frustration that their bosses were not up-to-date on technological and other key work matters. In fact three out of four of these young adults feel that they digest and understand information quicker than their supervisors.

The Millennials are looking for leadership and mentorship in the workplace. And they seem to be giving some of the leaders at work the benefit of the doubt, but they are frustrated. Indeed when it's all said and done, they would like for those above them in the organization to ask for their opinion and really desire their input.

Keep in mind, this generation is not lacking in confidence. They really believe they have something to offer in many areas, including the workplace.

And they are convinced they can help if we who are older and more experienced would just seek their advice on occasions. It is indeed a thought worth considering.

Attracting and Retaining Millennials in the Workplace

The topic of the Millennials in the workplace has been one of the most discussed and researched on this generation. It only makes sense. The investment of people is the most important and one of the most costly a business can make. We have attempted in this chapter to let the members of this generation who are at work tell their own stories and share their own experiences.

Though our concluding thoughts are far from exhaustive, we do believe the following six issues are key to establishing a healthy relationship between Millennials and their employers. Here is what they told us.

Issue 1: The basics of compensation and financial benefits are still important. Perhaps older generations have a tendency to think of Millennials as a totally different generation that has no commonalities with its predecessors. Such an assumption is faulty and fraught with risks.

This younger generation wants good pay and good benefits. And they will likely come fully prepared with industry averages and pay scales. Treat them fairly. They will know if you aren't.

Issue 2: Provide them clear expectations. If the pay and benefits don't meet their expectations, explain why the employer's numbers are different from their numbers. They will listen to a reasonable explanation. More than one Millennial told us that they came to a prospective employer with overzealous expectations about compensation. Most of them said that negotiations broke down because of the gap between the offer and the expectation. They wish now that the employer had taken time to explain the differential.

Millennials need clear guidelines in most areas of work, especially if it is their first full-time job. I (Thom) recently had a frank conversation with one of our younger employees. I told him that I had the perception that he was loose with his work hours and that he appeared to have a poor work ethic. He responded first with surprise and then quickly took action to change his work habits.

That response is typical of most Millennials. They respond well to guidance and even criticism, but they do need some clear guidelines and expectations. It will be worth the time and investment.

Similarly, this generation wants feedback. If it is limited to the customary annual review, they will become frustrated and restless. They need informal feedback on a regular basis.

Issue 3: Respect their personal and social relationships. Most of the Millennials are family focused. Most are social beings with a network of friends. They want a job that enhances those relationships rather than hinders them. My (Thom's) company has a "bring your child to work" day. It's a big hit with many of the employees. Now I'm considering, like many other employers, if I need to introduce a "bring your parents to work day." Many Millennials are still close to their parents.

While there are no cookie-cutter approaches to this issue, it would behoove organizational leaders to become creative about this desire of this generation. It could likely improve loyalty and enhance creativity.

Issue 4: Make it fun. Some employers cringe when they hear this suggestion. After all, the workplace is a place for serious business. Fun can be counterproductive.

Not so for the Millennials. Fun increases their productivity and loyalty. Of course, like any other issue, this one can be taken to an extreme. But most organizations are a long way from that extreme.

The Millennials with whom we spoke gave us a common characteristic of companies that have healthy fun: They have fun and joyous leaders. Jerome from Houston said it well: "A fun atmosphere at an organization is not so much a bunch of silly exercises as it is an attitude. And that attitude has to come from leaders in the organization."

Issue 5: Be a transparent leader. Millennials smell "fake" a mile away. They know when people aren't being real and sincere. They are attracted to organizations where the leaders are transparent and open. Those leaders are forthright with the people in the organization. They are at times willing to admit their struggles.

"I got a job offer with a 15 percent increase in pay with a company just a few blocks from where live," Sandra told us.

Sandra has just been in the workforce a little over a year. "It was tempting. I could use the money. But I really like where I am now. The company is great, and the leaders are real. I just am not so sure I could get that at the other company."

Issue 6: Listen to them. Most of the Millennials with whom we spoke didn't have a know-it-all attitude. But they did have some great insights and fresh perspectives. We wondered how many of their ideas were really entertained where they work.

This entire book has been an exercise in listening to Millennials. It has been one that has been both educational and enlightening. We both came away from our research richer in knowledge and deeper in relationships. The same thing can happen when we listen to the Millennials in the workplace. We get more loyal and productive employees because we listen. And we just might learn something new and creative in the process.

It's worth the effort.

CHAPTER 7

The Mediating Generation

N one of the Millennials mentioned it in our study.
Indeed, when we asked them about events in their life-
times that were markers, not one noted this incident.

Granted, the oldest Millennial was only eleven years old at
the time, and nearly half of the generation had yet to be born.
Perhaps it really doesn't define their generation. But the attitude
of many of the Millennials does seem to reflect the sentiments
expressed by this unfortunate time in America's history.

The date was March 3, 1991. Rodney Glen King was driving along the 210 Freeway in Los Angeles. He was speeding,
and later reports would indicate that he was under the influence of both alcohol and marijuana. Two Los Angeles Police
Department officers began to pursue King because he was

speeding. King panicked and led the officers and others on a high-speed chase for miles.

The events that followed are disputed. Did King try to attack LAPD officers after his vehicle was stopped? Did the officers provoke him to anger and fighting? Was King doing nothing and beaten for no good reason?

Not in dispute is what took place after Rodney King's vehicle was stopped. A bystander, George Holliday, videotaped four police officers beating King with the victim offering little resistance. Holliday would offer the LAPD the videotape, but they saw no need for it. Instead, a local television station took the footage. The scene would eventually be shown around the world, and King became the poster child for victims of police brutality.

Reaction was swift and negative around the nation as millions viewed the horrific beatings. King, an African-American, was attacked by four white police officers. From the perspective of the video footage, the attack was unprovoked toward a defenseless man. The rage in the nation was palpable.

A year later in 1992 all eyes were on a suburban state court in a predominantly white area. That was the scene for the trial of the four police officers accused of police brutality. The officers were tried and acquitted. The rage that had been simmering for a year began to boil over.

The Los Angeles riots that took place as a reaction to the verdict were some of the most destructive the city had known. More than fifty were killed. More than four thousand were injured. And the property damage in Los Angeles totaled over one billion dollars.

In the midst of the riots and suffering, Rodney King made a public statement. Though few recall most of his words, six words remain famous to this day: "Can we all just get along?"

Though the Millennials in our study did not mention the Rodney King event, most of them did use words similar to his: "Can we all just get along?" The Millennials are weary of the fights in our nation and world. They are tired of the polarization of views. They avoid the high-pitched shouts of opposing political forces. They are abandoning churches in great numbers because they see religion as divisive and argumentative.

They want to know why we can't all just get along.

It is not easy to assign a single adjective to this generation. If we were pushed, we might call them the "Mediating Generation." The great majority of them are weary of the polarization in families, in politics, in religion, and in relationships in general. This theme was evident throughout almost all phases of our study. Indeed it was so pervasive that it may be the defining issue for this generation for years to come.

Holding the Family Together

Jayne Anne has been married for three years. At age twenty-eight she seems much more mature than her years might indicate. Though we did not meet her husband, Rob, she assured us that his feelings about the family were at least as strong as hers.

"I guess I'm like many in my generation," she began. Her words were matter-of-fact and didn't betray great emotion. "My parents divorced when I was twelve. It was one of the most painful things I can imagine. I know losing a loved one is bad, but their divorce hurt as much as losing someone. Mom and Dad tried to hide their fights and arguments, but I'm no dummy. A twelve-year-old has a good idea what's going on."

She took a breath and continued, "I just returned from a trip to see Mom. We talked about the divorce, something we really hadn't done for years. Mom said that it was best to divorce so my brothers and I didn't have to live with all the fighting. I almost exploded in my reaction to her. I told her it was not best. I told her that it tore us up. I told her not ever to think that they did us a favor!"

Jayne Anne's composure disappeared. It was evident that the issue was still painful to her sixteen years later.

"I had to apologize to Mom," she now said softly. "I really hurt her by my outburst. I didn't mean to hurt her, but I was so tired of hearing how the divorce was best for us children. Don't they know that getting along and reconciling would have been best for us children? Were they really thinking of us?"

In chapter 3 we saw the centrality of the family to the Millennial Generation. Certainly numerous factors contribute to their focus. One factor, however, that was beyond doubt was this generation's laserlike focus on being a mediating force for the family. They desire to be different from the Baby Boomer Generation, whom they perceive to be "me focused." They want to do what it takes to hold families together. They are weary of the broken families and of the intense hurt they see in divided families.

"I am determined to hold my family together," Jayne Anne told us with resolve. "I know marriage takes a lot of work. I know it means I have to sacrifice self for my husband and my children. But I will do it. I am doing it. Nothing is more important to me than holding my family together."

We certainly can't predict if the Millennial Generation will be the generation that reverses the trends of broken families, but early evidence seems positive. Those who are married and those who are not are determined now and in the future to keep marriages intact and families together. They just want everyone to get along.

One rather interesting indication of the Millennials' attitude about marriage and family actually came out of our questions to them about leadership. We asked them to describe the type of person from whom they would like to learn. Not only did the response surprise us, but also the overwhelming nature of the response surprised us. They told us that they would like to learn from people who have long-term successful marriages. In fact, 91 percent held these people up as their heroes and their life examples. We doubt that most Baby Boomers would have looked to long-term married couples as their heroes thirty years ago.

They want families to get along. They want spouses to get along. And, at least to this point, the Millennials seem to be on track to do something about it.

The Mediating Motive in Same-sex Marriages

We noted earlier in this book that Millennials as a majority approve same-sex marriages. The specific statement we gave them was: "I see nothing wrong with the same gender getting married." The split between agree and disagree was 61 percent to 39 percent. It is particularly fascinating to see some of the motives and comments behind the numbers.

First, religious conviction played a large role in the response. For example, among those who were Evangelicals, 84 percent did not approve of same-sex marriages. Evangelicals included those who affirmed several specific doctrinal statements. On another level, among those who attend church, 62 percent did not approve of same-sex marriages.

As you would expect, the numbers are dramatically different for those who don't have strong religious convictions. Among those who do not attend church, 74 percent approve of same-sex marriages. And among those who stated that they have no religious affiliation, 85 percent approve.

When we heard from the latter group, the majority who approve same-sex marriages, we heard a common theme. They are tired of the conflict between the two groups on opposite sides of this volatile issue. Notes Jon from Milwaukee: "I just get sick and tired of all the shrill voices on both sides of this. We just need to leave people alone and let it be a private issue. We don't need to impose our values on someone and tell them what they can and can't do it in the privacy of their own homes."

Of course those with convictions about same-sex relation-ships, particularly those with religious convictions, expressed strong disagreement. Monty of Austin, Texas, said: "It's not really a matter of imposing our views; it's the view of the Bible. I'm not telling someone what they can or can't do; I'm just tell-ing them what God says in the Bible."

Even in the Millennial Generation, the debate on same-sex relationships is polarizing. But there is little doubt that those who are open to such relationships have made significant gains with this generation. And one of the primary reasons the gains have been made is a perception among many that we just need first to get along. Opposing same-gender marriages and relationships is thus seen to be divisive, something the mediat-ing generation would like to avoid.

The Respectful Generation

An absolutely amazing and rewarding finding in our study was the level of respect the Millennials have for others. We wish we had comparable numbers for previous generations because we suspect that the results for this generation would be at its highest levels in a century.

At the risk of redundancy, we need to remember that the Millennials represent a group of young adults who are weary of divisiveness and polarized views. Many commented to us that they will not watch news channels simply because they are fed up with the shrill voices of some commentators and guests.

It should not, therefore, be a big surprise that respect is a significant issue for this generation. For them respect is the willingness to listen, to hear carefully what someone else has to say. It does not mean that you agree with everyone on everything. But it does mean that you will treat them with respect.

On the matter of mutual respect, the Millennials were unequivocal. It was nearly unanimous: 97 percent said they respect others who respect them. And 64 percent agreed strongly, a high number for those with strong feelings on any of the questions we asked them.

"If we would just show respect toward others, this world would be a better place," said Amy, a twenty-nine-year-old software consultant from Reno, Nevada. "It seems like all we do is argue and fight these days."

She then became more emotive as she talked about politicians. "Have you noticed how almost all politicians show no respect for one another?" she asked rhetorically. "Then have you noticed how congress has the lowest approval ratings of any group? It's because they are a bunch of jerks and thugs that scream at one another. They show no respect so they get no respect. I hope my generation votes them all out of office!"

Amy's opinions were indicative of her peers. This generation is a mediating generation where most insist that we respect one another. In fact, this issue of respecting one another was one of the few where all subgroups of the Millennials had the same strong opinions. Though much good research has been done on this generation, this issue of respect and mediation may be one that has been largely overlooked.

In chapter 3 we saw the incredible bond that exists between the Millennials and their parents. But this level of respect for older generations was not limited to their immediate family. One of the most telling responses to a statement we received was connected to the respect the Millennials demonstrate for all older generations. In this particular statement, we used the superlative "great," thinking it might diminish the positive responses. Our assumptions were wrong.

In response to the statement, "I tend to have great respect for people in older generations," an incredible 94 percent agreed. Again we wish we had comparable numbers for earlier generations. Still we know that the results could not have been much higher than 94 percent!

Rarely in our study did we see such overwhelming numbers. Some in my (Thom's) Baby Boomer generation may remember our condescending views of older adults. Many of us did not respect those older than us. Indeed many of us showed contempt for those older than us.

As we attempted to discern why attitudes shifted from the Baby Boomers to the Millennials, we found at least three reasonable explanations. First, the relationship between Millennials and their parents established a bond with and respect for older persons that was able to transcend family relationships to others.

Kevin is from Louisville, Kentucky. He demonstrates to us a maturity that seems beyond his twenty-six years. And he speaks with both passion and respect about his admiration for his parents and their generation.

"I really do love hanging out with my mom and dad," he told us. "Not all of my friends have the same kind of relationship with their parents that I do, so I really appreciate what I've got. I've also learned to enjoy their friends. I know their generation was messed up in many ways, but you've got to appreciate how most of them relate to my age group. They've really tried to connect with us younger guys, so we have grown up appreciating and respecting them too."

Kevin explains further how that relationship makes him respect older persons in general. "I really never knew anything but a good relationship with older persons," he said. "I guess I just expected that the mutual respect my parents and I have for each other would hold true with most older adults. And you know, it has for the most part. I really do respect those older than me."

Though we are reticent to overplay the significance of 9-11 and the subsequent war on terrorism, it does seem to be a defining event for the largest generation in America's history. We certainly heard an abundance of comments from them about those tragic days. Keep in mind that the range of ages of this generation on September 11, 2001, was roughly one year old to twenty-one years old. While we can't expect the youngest members of this generation to recall that day, our surveys only included those whose ages were ten to twenty-one years old on 9-11. They certainly remember that day, often in vivid details.

It seems as though the events of 9-11 gave the Millennials a sober view of life. For many it gave them a perspective of the brevity of life. For that reason many in this generation want to make the most of relationships. They know that life ends, sometimes tragically. They, therefore, are typically desirous to make the most of all relationships, including with those who are older than they are.

Alicia of Hartford, Connecticut, stated that truth succinctly. "Life is short," she said. "I am determined to enjoy the best of every relationship I can."

For the Millennials that certainly includes those older than them.

A third scenario further explains the Millennials' desire to have strong bonds with older persons. It goes back to our thesis of this chapter and our discoveries of this generation. They are a mediating generation. They want to get along with others if at all possible. They are tired of divisiveness and conflicts. They want to get along with everyone, especially those who are older.

The Baby Boomers were skeptical of others and often caustic in their attitudes. Not so the Millennials. They are largely forgiving and relational. They want to get along. And they have trouble understanding why the rest of the generations don't feel the same.

The Mediating Green Generation

We anticipated that at least an entire chapter of this book would be devoted to the Millennials and the environment. Many of our questions in our study certainly directed the conversation that way. But in the final analysis we were reticent to call the Millennials either "the environmental generation" or "the green generation."

Let us be clear. The Millennials *are* concerned about environmental issues. But their concerns were much less than we anticipated. And some of their responses did surprise us. Look at just a few of the examples:

- A majority of the generation feels that many of their peers go overboard on environmental issues.
- Just 16 percent indicated that a candidate's environmental conscience has a major impact on how they vote.
- Only 23 percent are strongly concerned with having a job that has a positive impact on the environment.

We will unpack these and other related matters shortly. For now, let us state the overall theme of the Millennials and environmentalism. First, this generation *is* concerned about the environment but not to the degree or with the passion some have supposed. Second, the Millennials are even more interested in creating a consensus on environmental issues.

Don't read over the previous sentence too quickly. The Millennials are even more interested in creating a *consensus* on environmental issues. Yes, they are concerned about the environment. But they are also concerned about the polarization engendered by this issue. Once again the Millennials are demonstrating that they are the mediating generation.

Let's look deeper at the environmental issue since it seems to be a point of discussion about this generation. And let's see how the majority of Millennials are attempting to build a consensus on the topic.

First, we need to be clear that Millennials are indeed a green generation. When we asked them if it was their generation's responsibility to clean up the environment, an overwhelming 87 percent responded affirmatively. But we were surprised that only 41 percent agreed strongly on this issue. As we followed up with further questions, we once again saw that the mediating desires of the Millennials showed up.

"I answered that question positively," said Karen of Albany, Georgia. "But I did not say I strongly agreed." She noticed that we were perplexed at her response, so she elaborated. "While I believe my generation has a responsibility to clean up the mess, I don't believe it's all our responsibility. That attitude kind of makes it an 'us versus them' mentality. We need to be working together instead of having some kind of messianic complex where we think it's up to us and us alone. That divides rather than unites people."

Once again, hear the tone of reconciliation in the responses. The mediating generation works to bring people together on issues, even hot-button issues like the environment.

This attitude was never more apparent than our question about who is responsible for harming the environment. It would seem that, whether by negligence, ignorance, or intentionality, only previous generations could be blamed. But the Millennials are not quick to blame those who came before them.

Granted, 74 percent did agree that previous generations hold some responsibility for the state of the environment. But only one-fourth of the Millennials strongly agreed. The difference? Once again many members of this generation are reticent to place blame for fear of polarization.

"Sure they messed up the planet some," Mandy said with little emotion. She is a twenty-two-year-old college senior living near Tempe, Arizona. "But I think most of the mess was done without knowing the damage they were doing. Instead of placing blame, we need to be finding ways to work together."

Once again the key issue for the Millennials is working together. They see the blame game as having no value. To the contrary, for them it is wasted energy that takes our focus off what really needs to be done.

We also asked the Millennials to evaluate themselves on the environmental issue. They were split on the statement: "Many people in my generation go overboard on environmental issues." More than half, 54 percent, agreed with that assessment. But the feelings were not strong either way on the statement: 18 percent agreed strongly, and only 10 percent disagreed strongly.

We caught Lisa just after she returned from her honeymoon. The twenty-seven-year-old Nebraska native summarized it well for her generation: "Sure, there are a few real environmental wackos in our generation. They are the ones that seem to get the attention. But they really don't speak for most of us. Most of us want to improve the environment by working together. Some extremists on both sides of the issue will make the news, but that's not where most of us are."

Environmental issues are important, but most Millennials are not single-issue voters. When we asked them if one of the key factors in voting for a political candidate was his environmental conscience, only 16 percent agreed strongly, while another 51 percent somewhat agreed. Again, it is an issue, but not the defining issue.

We received a similar response when we asked these young adults if they will choose a job in an organization that benefits the environment: 23 percent agreed strongly and another 50 percent somewhat agreed. The green issue is significant, but it is not the all-defining issue as stereotyped by some.

The essence of the Millennials' perspective on the environment is that, undoubtedly, the issue is important to them. They recognize that we all must be good stewards of this planet. But they are not extremists in their views. They realize that the best way to go green is to work together. Most of them have little patience with the blame game. They see it as polarizing and self-defeating.

Nate summed it well for his generation: "The environment is an important issue for us. Undoubtedly it's more important for me than it was for my parents when they were my age. But there is a lot to do to clean up the environment and keep it clean. We need to work together to get it done. That's the only way."

The mediating generation has spoken again.

The Serving Generation

Unlike some who have written on the Millennials, we are encouraged and hopeful about this generation. No generation is perfect and all have their flaws. But there is much about the Millennials to like.

As we have noted repeatedly in this chapter, the majority of Millennials have a desire to bring people together. We have noted that reality in their families, in their marriages, in their relationships with others, and in the way they respond to such hot-button issues as same-sex marriage and the environment.

Indeed, if the second largest generation, the Baby Boomers, were the "me generation," it is not unreasonable to call the largest generation, the Millennials, "the serving generation." These nearly seventy-eight million young people as a whole are not focused as much on self as they are the good and unity of others.

Those who are trying to connect with the Millennials would do well to focus on how they can serve others and society. Most of them truly have a focus away from self. Most of them want to make a difference and serve others. They once again demonstrate their desire to bring people together by serving them.

Three out of four Millennials told us clearly that they desired to serve others in society. Only 4 percent said emphatically that such is not their motive. This attitude was pervasive in all sub-groups. The motive was even stronger in groups that claimed a religious affiliation and strongest among those who were self-described as Christians, born again, and Evangelicals.

Though it was not their primary motive in choosing a job, Millennials were more likely to work or desire to work in a place that contributed to society. In fact, seven out of ten who are currently employed felt that the place they work makes a significant contribution to society.

We don't want to overstate the altruistic motives of the Millennials. They are not clones of Mother Teresa. But they do have a desire to be a mediating force in society. Some of their approaches may well accomplish the goals they have in mind. They seek to work together rather than place blame on others. They seek family unity and are willing to make the sacrifices to keep the family together. And many of them want to serve others. There are sufficient altruistic motives that we remain optimistic about this generation and how they will affect our nation and world. But, for the sake of full disclosure, we did find some issues that might seem less than noble. Let's take a few moments and look at the other side of the Millennials.

The Other Side of the Millennials

In this chapter we have been rather lavish in our praise of the Millennials. They are the generation that seeks to bring people together. They work toward family unity. They work at jobs that make a difference in society. They are concerned about the environment, but they avoid extremism on both sides of the issue. They are a serving generation, putting others' needs before themselves.

Though we are generally positive about this generation, we have to be careful not to paint a perfect picture. Some of the responses we received in our study were not totally altruistic. Let us share a few.

Money and wealth are still important. We are not suggesting that the desires to make money and accumulate wealth are unhealthy motives. Those with capitalistic motives and actions have fueled much of the economic growth of our nation. We just wanted to be clear that the Millennials are not all about sacrifice and giving away wealth.

At this point you may be surprised that more than eight out of ten Millennials have a specific goal to become at least modestly wealthy. And some have goals well beyond modest wealth. "I want to be stinking rich," Steve told us. We are not certain about the odor of wealth, but we understand his point. "I can do more for my family, me, and others if I have lots of money. I am working hard toward that goal." Indeed, most of the Millennials saw no conflict in their motives for service and unity and in their motive for wealth, whether it is modest wealth or "stinking" wealth.

They have some resentment about their unused potential. The Millennials are impatient. They know life is short, and they don't want to delay. They want to make a difference now. The issue of unused potential is huge for them; 85 percent felt that they have a *lot* of unused potential.

"I can't understand why I'm always being told to be patient," noted Katie. The twenty-seven-year-old lady from Bloomington, Indiana, felt that she could be doing much more. "It really irks me in my job right now," she said. "My bosses tell me that my time will come, but I don't understand it. I am so much more qualified than some of the older guys there."

Katie paused for a moment. She wasn't really angry, but she was frustrated. "It seems like, since I graduated from college, I have been told to wait my turn," she continued. "I just don't understand why. I feel like I have so much unused potential."

Katie speaks for most of her generation. This is the generation that thinks they can do something great. In fact, 96 percent feel they can do something great, and 60 percent feel strongly about it. They are ready to do something. They are ready to make a difference. And they are ready now.

3. **Some of their resentment is directed toward the Baby Boomers.** For the most part, the Millennials' relationship with the other large generation, the Baby Boomers, is healthy. We have noted how their generally healthy relationship with their Boomer parents has translated into a good relationship between the two generations.

Still, some of the Millennials do believe the Baby Boomers are holding them back from accomplishing their goals. About one-half of those we surveyed told us that Boomers who know them tend to doubt their abilities because of their relative youth. Only 15 percent really felt strongly about this issue so it's not a huge deal for the Millennials. But it is just one other indicator that the world of the largest generation in America is not perfect.

The Strange Matter of Attitude and Spirituality

We delve into matters of spirituality and religious affiliation in detail in chapter 10. As a precursor, we will note that

65 percent of the Millennials expressed a broadly Christian preference. As we will discuss later, we have good reason to believe that the actual number who are Christians is much smaller.

Only 6 percent indicated they were atheists, those who do not believe any god exists. Another 8 percent claimed to be agnostics, those who have some doubt about the existence of a god. Another 14 percent noted no religious preference at all. So we can say in rough terms that three out of ten have no religious identity.

But seven out of ten do have a religious identity, and most of those are Christians. Only a few noted they were Jewish, Hindu, Muslim, Buddhist, Wiccan, or pagan. Our point is that most did have a religious identity, dominated by Christians.

Here is our dilemma. If most religions, particularly Christianity, are identified by their service to others, and if most Millennials desire to serve others, why is not the vast majority of this generation serving actively in a local church? Less than one-fourth of all the respondents indicated that they are in a religious service each week.

Indeed the great numbers of Millennials have some spiritual identity, but they are avoiding organized religions like local churches in great numbers as well. From our earlier research, we found that this generation is likely the most "unchurched" generation in over a century.

Why?

Listen to Tabitha. She represents the sentiments of most of her peers in the Millennial Generation.

"I guess I would call myself a Christian," she began. "My parents went to church sometimes, and they always told me that we were Christians. Now I don't practice my faith that much, but if you had to label me, that's probably where I'd be."

We then asked Tabitha if she attended a church on a regular basis. "Actually no," she began. "I did attend church for several months about three years ago. But the more I got to know people in the church, the more I heard about infighting and fussing. That made me notice how negative church people and preachers are in general. You know, it seems like every time I read about a Christian leader, he's telling people what he's against. It just all seems so negative."

Her excursion took us down a path where many of the respondents in our study traveled. We could anticipate the rest of Tabitha's conversation.

"I'm a pretty spiritual person," she then told us. "I pray to God. Sometimes I try to read the Bible, though it's kind of hard to understand. But I'm just not too interested in organized religion. It seems like all those people talk about is what they don't like and how everything's screwed up. That's not for me. Things are tough enough without having to put up with all that negativity."

Religion is thus viewed by many of the Millennials as just another divisive force in the world. More specifically, they see problems with organized and institutional religion. The Millennials are the mediating generation and, from the perspective of many, organized religion leads to negativity and conflict. And, as we will see in greater detail in chapter 10, most of this generation avoid churches and other institutional forms of religion for that reason.

Some Closing Thoughts on the Mediating Generation

After our research was complete on the Millennial Generation, and after we synthesized and interpreted most of the data, we came to a pleasant conclusion: we really like this generation. Most of the responses were well thought, and the follow-up interviews were typically energetic and fun.

Yeah, we like this generation.

We know that, out of seventy-eight million persons, there will be a few million less-than-pleasant people. We know that this generation has its problems.

But we still like them.

We did not anticipate that we would have a chapter called "The Mediating Generation," but the data drove us in that direction. And before we go to the next chapter and the trendier topic of their relationship with the media, we need to make five final observations about the Millennials and their propensity toward mediation.

1. **There are many peacemakers among the Millennials.** This generation has known conflict from the time they were born. They know no other world than 24-7 news coverage and opinionated, shrill voices. They only know politicians who scream at one another and show little decorum and respect toward one another. They see the religious landscape covered with angry leaders who denounce everything, at least from their perspectives.

They are tired of the divisions. They are weary of the polarization. They are looking for leaders who will bring people together. They are looking for common courtesy and civility. And they are willing, even eager, to do their part toward this end.

The Millennials are determined to keep families together. The peacemaking traits characteristic of many of the Millennials found its way into families. The reason is straightforward. Many in this generation are the products of broken families. They have experienced the pain of having a mom and dad living in two homes in two states. They have witnessed firsthand the fights and conflicts taking place in too many homes. Some have been victims of abuse.

The mediating generation wants to reverse these trends. Most of them are entering young adulthood with idealistic notions about their families and future families. But that idealism is coupled with a realism that knows healthy marriages and healthy families require a lot of work. Again, we can't predict if we will see significant improvement in divorce rates, child abuse, and general family conflict. But we won't be surprised if it happens. The majority of this generation is determined to do so.

The Millennials are not without convictions. It may seem on the surface that this generation is a "peace at all costs" generation. That is not so. They have clear convictions across the political, religious, and ideological spectrum. They have convictions about hot-button issues like same-gender marriages and environmental actions.

Certainly their tendency will be to bring factions together, to avoid conflict if at all possible. But they are not unrealistic. The Millennials know that disagreements will always be present. They are more concerned, however, about the tone of the disagreements. They are impatient with shrill voices and lack of civility. We began this chapter with the Rodney King question: "Can we all just get along?" For the Millennials that question does not mean that they leave their convictions at the door. It does mean, though, that we speak with civility and that we treat one another with respect.

They have learned to respect others from their Boomer parents. The Boomers get much well-deserved blame for the mess of our society today. The purpose of this book is not to pile on that generation. That's another book in the making.

We can give the Boomer generation at least one accolade. Most of the Boomer parents have had good relationships with their children. That relationship of mutual respect is now a part of the generational personality of the Millennials. And it will likely bode well for this generation as they prepare to lead in the twenty-first century.

The status quo is in trouble. The Millennials are an impatient generation. They are ready to make large-scale changes if they deem it necessary. They are ready to vote out shrill and argumentative politicians. They don't like the inwardly focused institutional church. They are ready for businesses to make the necessary changes to be a positive force for society. They don't understand why educational institutions are so slow to adapt, and they are ready to move to those that do.

They are impatient. They understand the brevity of life, and they don't want to wait. Change has been a reality in their lives from their birth to now. They won't stand still.

The Millennials are coming.

We had better get ready or get out of the way.

CHAPTER 8

The Millennials and Media

I (Thom) love oldies music.

The 1960s produced the best music. The Beatles, the Beach Boys, the Monkees, the Mamas and the Papas, and the Drifters gained popularity during this decade. The 1960s was the decade of the British music invasion. The Beatles, the Rolling Stones, the Who, and the Animals found their place in the American music scene. The 1960s was the decade of Woodstock. Although not my favorite, artists such as Jimi Hendrix, the Grateful Dead, Janis Joplin, and Creedence Clearwater Revival reached the top of music charts across the nation.

My sons often joke that I could sing, talk, and answer trivia about 1960s music all day. Their joking just might be truth. While my love for oldies has remained, the way I listen to them has changed. It started with vinyl records. I love the distinct sound of music playing from vinyl records accompanied by the occasional pop or click. While I did own a few, I never really got excited about eight-track tapes. It was too hard to give up my records. Cassette tapes, on the other hand, were wonderful. I could actually listen to the songs I wanted to hear in the car.

The arrival of compact discs (CDs) provided a new format to music. As far as listening, nothing much changed from CDs for me. The rise of digital music has made a world of difference though. The ability to take a media music player, such as my iPhone, and listen to music wherever I want is incredible. If there is a song I want to hear, I can download it that moment. Music has become instantaneous.

I have managed to stay with the changes in music media. I was not always so adaptable. I received my first laptop when I was a dean of a seminary. The laptop also provided me personal Internet access for the first time. My first laptop and Internet experience were unforgettable, mostly because Danny Akin (another dean at the seminary) was there with me.

Dr. Akin and I sat in an office of the school's technology department. A lady, we will call her Sally, was going to give us a guided tour of the World Wide Web. As she entered the room, she greeted us, "Good morning, Dr. Rainer and Dr. Akin. My name is Sally. I am going to give you a brief tour of the functions of the Internet. Let's begin by opening your Netscape Browser. Once your browser has loaded, you will notice the seminary's home page."

At this point Dr. Akin and I looked at our laptops, at each other, at Sally, and then back at our laptops. Sally continued, "By now you will notice the '.edu' domain in your address bar. The Web site is usually preceded by 'http' in the address bar as well. The 'http' usually remains when you are going to a new Web site, but the '.edu' will change. These are all parts of the 'URL.' The 'URL' recognizes the location and type of resource on the Web."

Dr. Akin and I started to smile. Sally was obviously encouraged by our enthusiasm as she continued. "The beginning of your 'URL' will usually start with 'www' after the 'http.' The 'www' stands for . . . Well, I am sure that you know that. Sorry if I am teaching you in an elementary way. To go to a new Web site, you simply need to change the input field after the 'www.' Go ahead and enter 'irs' after the 'www.' Once that is done, change the domain to '.gov.'" Sally stopped and looked at us. This time when she looked at us, she realized we had just been looking at her and smiling.

Sally inquired, "Why have you not been entering the information?" I looked over at Dr. Akin who just stared back at me. I turned to Sally and asked, "How do you turn the thing on?" The look on Sally's face was priceless. I wish I had my iPhone then to take a picture. A lot has changed since 1995.

A lot will continue to change in the world of media and technology. And we (Thom and Jess) understand how quickly that change occurs. By the time this book reaches the hands of our readers, the media mentioned in this chapter might already be dated. The data we gathered from the Millennials about media will serve as a point of comparison though. The Millennials have opinions about media now that will have an impact for years to come.

Before we learn about the Millennials' thoughts and attitudes about media and where they believe it's headed, let's do a brief overview of the history of media. Although a short history lesson, there is still a lot to uncover.

(A Brief) History of Media

Media is the transmission of information from a source to a recipient. It is often referred to as mass media or the transmission of information to the general public. There is no exact date of media's origination. Ancient dramas are often viewed as the first public distribution of information. Since there is no distinct point in history, any type of information distributed in rhetoric form could be viewed as the starting point for media.

Written information is found throughout history. Not until 1453, however, with the invention of the movable-type printing press did written materials begin to circulate in a more widespread fashion. Large amounts of new publications were delivered to the general public starting in the seventeenth century. North American publications began in Boston in the early 1700s. New York and Philadelphia soon followed suit and produced weekly newspapers. The print industry quickly became the primary source for news and information.

Movies, or film, made their debut around 1900. Film was originally introduced to the American public with no sound.

For the first thirty years of film, often called the silent film era, films were presented with either live musicians, a narrator, or in silence. Around 1930 technology was created to record sound and video simultaneously. Movies were shown on film reels to an audience.

In the 1980s the way Americans were able to watch movies changed. The film reel gave way to the videocassette recorder (VCR). The introduction of the VCR to moviegoers enabled them to enjoy a movie from the comfort of their own home. The introduction of the digital video disc or DVD provided a new and high quality format to watch movies. People can now watch 3D movies at home as well as the movie theater.

Shortly after the introduction of film, another form of media quickly came on the scene. Radio technology was developed in the 1800s. Its development reached a point around 1920 where it was used for the general public. Hundreds of radio stations were set up in just a few years across the United States. There has been little development of the radio since its inception. Probably the biggest change was the use of satellites to transmit audio. Satellite radio created an almost endless range of broadcasting. Two other major changes that came in the twenty-first century: Internet and digital radio were developed as an alternate transmission means other than traditional FM radio waves.

The creation of television is not credited to one individual. Many engineers and innovators had their hands in the creation of television. Television began around the turn of the twentieth century. Different methods of producing television surfaced, but ultimately electronic television (the version we use today) was the method of choice.

The first regularly scheduled television broadcast in the United States was in 1928. Broadcasting continued but did not gain a significant viewer base until the late 1940s. What really increased the television as a media was the availability of television sets. Unlike radios, televisions were expensive. Companies eventually found a way to produce inexpensive ones. In 1950 approximately 10 percent of American households owned a television set. Just ten years later almost 90 percent of American families had one in their homes.

As television grew in popularity, television sets and broadcasting increased in quality. Cable and satellite television entered the media marketplace in the 1970s. More channels and more choices caused television to become the dominant media source until the 1990s. Newspapers and radios still remained a viable news source, but the appeal of seeing and hearing new information took precedence in the media world.

Any attempt to describe the history of the Internet would prove futile. The complexity of not only the Internet itself but also those who lay claim to its creation, is far too great to address in this setting. The Internet began as a means for different computer networks to communicate to one another. E-mail, or electronic messages, submitted from one network to another, started in the 1960s.

The Internet's growth began in the 1980s. Two main uses of the Internet surfaced during this time. The first was e-mail. The second was search engines. Developers saw the need to organize the information of this massively growing network. Search engines were created in order to help users find information more easily. The Internet saw a massive increase in users in the mid-1990s. Personal computers became affordable, resulting in more and more unique users surfing the World Wide Web. In just a short amount of time, the Internet has accumulated more than 230 million users. The Internet is *the* media source today.

While much more could be addressed about the history of media, this brief lesson sets the stage for the rest of this chapter. The Millennials entered into the media scene during a time of great technological advancements. This generation is unique in that, unlike previous generations, they do not know a world without technology and media.

A Personal Media Pilgrimage

My (Jess') pilgrimage began with the Oregon Trail. Many of my Millennial peers know exactly what I am talking about. For those who do not, let me explain. I did not make my way from the Missouri Valley to the Oregon Territory by ox and wagon. Not literally anyway. *The Oregon Trail* was one of the first major educational video games, often played in schools. The game emulated a real-life journey across the western United States with a team of oxen pulling a wagon. Hunting, sickness, broken wagon wheels, and even death were a part of the journey. This video game did more than educate children about life in the mid-1800s. It helped America's youth to develop a passion for media, technology, and electronics.

The Oregon Trail did change my perspective on computers while I was in fourth grade. It was not that I was merely playing a video game. For as long as I can remember, I always played video games. I remember my first video-game console, the Atari. I also remember the consoles that followed: Nintendo, Sega, Super Nintendo, Dreamcast, Playstation 1, 2, & 3, Gamecube, Xbox, and Wii. *The Oregon Trail* showed that a computer was not just for spreadsheets and data input. A computer could be used for pleasure, not just business.

With my newfound enjoyment, I decided to start exploring my family's home computer. The Tandy home computer, which was sold through Radio Shack, became an instant source of learning for me. I spent a lot of time on our family's Tandy making music, painting pictures, playing games, and sometimes doing homework. Watching my dad occasionally use a typewriter or write longhand already seemed ancient. Even now, thinking that my dad wrote his first books with a pen and paper seems strange.

Earlier in this chapter, my dad wrote about his first use of the Internet and a laptop. I remember the day he brought home that laptop. Almost two inches thick, it had a trackball (or mouse) that attached to the side of the keyboard under the black-and-white screen. We unhooked the phone and plugged the phone line into the computer. After the screeches and hums of the computer connecting to the Internet, we were welcomed to the World Wide Web. I do not exactly remember what we searched for, but I remember my whole family watching in amazement.

Several years later after technology quickly upgraded, my dad eventually bought a family laptop. After signing up with America Online (AOL), I received my first e-mail address while in middle school. As an eleven-year-old with personal Internet access, I began to trade e-mail addresses with classmates. While we sent few e-mails, we did embrace a new technology, instant messaging. Instant message (or AIM) became the main source for my computer use. The ability to chat with multiple friends at the same time with little effort became an instant hit. The popularity of AIM set the tone for big changes in communication, especially for the Millennials.

Instant messaging faded out of my common communication methods with the arrival of text messaging. I received my first cell phone about the time I reached eighth grade. While I enjoyed the ability to talk at anytime, I loved the ability to text message on my phone. Conversations now existed in small spurts of words combined with abbreviations and acronyms. This is where my generation first learned to communicate with brevity.

My departure for college prompted the purchase of my own personal computer. While having my own computer did not change any of my views on technology, it did illustrate the widespread ability to obtain powerful technology. Computers were no longer confined to classrooms of universities and schools but found themselves in the hands of America's youth.

As more Millennials obtained computers, more doors opened for my generation to make their impact on the Internet. One of the first major impacts was file sharing. File sharing was most commonly used to obtain music from other computers. Napster was the most notorious for peer-to-peer file sharing. The influx of digital music led to the popularity of MP3 players, and most notably the iPod. File sharing and digital music changed the way we obtained and listened to music. The days of CDs and cassettes were gone.

The iPod introduced my generation to what would soon be the favorite technology for many of us. Apple brand products appeal to my generation. The ease of use, the reliability, and the cosmetic design make anything Apple desirable. While my take on Millennials and Apple is purely anecdotal, I do believe the constant rise in Apple stock price since 2002 indicates the power of Apple. An Apple product introduced in 2010, the iPad, sold three million units in less than three months or one unit every 2.3 seconds.

While my generation's desire for the best technology continues to grow, our desire for the best communication method also grew. It is hard to put a start date on social media, but Web sites such as MySpace and Facebook gained a lot of popularity during the early to mid-2000s. Social media gave Millennials the ability to not only talk but also to see and hear about the lives of our friends. We could find connections with not-so-close friends that would otherwise be unknown if not for social media.

It is fascinating to think back to elementary school and the days of *The Oregon Trail*. It makes me realize the uniqueness of my generation. I often distinguish the breaks in my childhood by technological advancements. Previous generations could not even fathom this line of thought. These generations may refer to their lives as before and after the introduction of social media. For the Millennials, it is all about the latest and greatest form of media.

Technologically Savvy

Millennials are synonymous with technology. Those who speak of the Millennial Generation often view technology and media as one of their defining characteristics. This comparison is warranted. Jess' connection to technology and media is a part of his upbringing, as he just illustrated.

Before we move any further, let us explain the use of our terminology. The terms *media* and *technology* are often used interchangeably. Although different terms, there is a correlation. Technology can be viewed as the means, while media is the ends. New delivery methods of media will result from technological advances. The Millennial Generation uses multiple forms of media.

The Millennials' use of media is a result of their knowledge of technology. It's almost innate. Ask a Millennial to locate his or her computer's IP address. Most Millennials would know where to find it or at least be able to locate the information on how to find it. Millennials are technologically savvy.

Since the Millennials are so in tune with how technology works, they are the ones who snatch up the first release of the latest technology. Right? We wanted to verify that perception of the Millennials.

The technology adoption life cycle is a bell curve that gives percentages of how quickly people adopt a new technology. There are five categories:

- Innovators (2.5 percent)
- Early Adopters (13.5 percent)
- Early Majority (34 percent)
- Late Majority (34 percent)
- Laggards (16 percent)

Innovators are highly educated and wealthy. Early adopters are young, educated, and socially active. The early majority is conservative but open to change. The late majority is older and less socially active. The laggards are skeptical and are often the least educated and the oldest. By definition, the Millennials fall into the early adopters stage.

So how do the Millennials view themselves within the technology adoption life cycle? We asked our respondents to agree or disagree with the following statement: "I am usually among the first people to acquire products featuring new technology." Those who disagreed with the statement totaled 46 percent. Almost half of the Millennials do not see themselves as early technology adopters. They see others snatching the newest technology up before they do.

There is one technology that the Millennials always have their hands on, literally. Video-game consoles are a part of an industry that pulled in more than twenty billion dollars in revenue in 2008. There is a risk in relating a generation to one form of media or technology. Technology changes too rapidly. But at this point in American generations, not one other generation has embraced a technology like the Millennials have embraced video games.

The expansion of online video gaming has only increased the level of technological involvement for the Millennials. Virtual peer-to-peer interaction has changed some of the Millennials' social interaction. Friendships are built over the Internet while playing video games. Millennials use online video games as a means of both entertainment and communication.

Online video games may be one of the newest methods of communication for the Millennials, but it is definitely not the only method. The Millennial Generation employs multiple personal communication methods, both conventional and unconventional. Let's see how the Millennials embrace this form of media.

The New World of Communication

In your personal communications (with family and friends), what form of communication do you use most frequently when you're not actually with the other person? That is the exact question we asked the Millennials. Here is how they responded:

- Phone (39 percent)
- Texting (37 percent)
- E-mail (16 percent)
- IM (Instant Message) (7 percent)
- Letters (1 percent)

Thom and Jess both analyzed how the Millennials communicate. And each author saw a different surprising find in the Millennials' response.

I (Jess) am surprised about the rankings of the forms of communication. If I would have taken the time to rank my prediction of these results, phone would have ranked third. Both texting and e-mail would have moved up one spot each. It is even more surprising to see texting as less popular than talking on the phone. When I think about how my friends and I communicate, a text message is used the majority of the time. It is faster, easier, and to the point. It eliminates small talk.

I also recognize myself as an older Millennial. Understanding that I use text messaging as much as I do, it would only be natural that the younger Millennials would use texting even more. In my opinion this statistic is dynamic. I believe more and more Millennials will use texting as a primary source of communication.

I (Thom) enjoy talking numbers with my sons. They all have undergraduate majors in finance, and they all have taken statistic courses. And they will always bring a slightly different perspective to the same information at which I am looking. Jess' surprise is based on observation of his peers and of himself. Just as Jess' observation shows his (young) age, my observation shows my (old) age.

I used to write letters growing up all the time. I would write my aunts and uncles. I would write people in my community. I would occasionally write to my friends. A letter has a sense of personal touch that is not found in other forms of communication. While e-mails and texting can have personalization, the time spent writing a letter creates additional value. I am surprised to see that only 1 percent of Millennials use letters as an alternate primary method of communication. Statistically speaking, letters are virtually nonexistent.

My belief is that the Millennial Generation understands the value of written communication. It appears the time spent for a handwritten form of communication just does not fit within the fast-paced lifestyle of the Millennials. Those Millennials who do find the time to write a letter or quick thank-you note might find themselves better positioned, especially in the workplace. A thank-you note to a Baby Boomer could make the difference between landing the job or not.

Thom and Jess' surprises to the way Millennials prefer to communicate illustrate how communication has changed from generation to generation. It is no surprise that the cell phone has played a major impact in this change. Cell phones have only been around for the better part of twenty years. Yet their contribution to changing the way America operates is undeniable.

Cell phones have reached a point of extreme importance in American culture. We asked the Millennials how vital their cell phone is to their lives. Seventy-three percent of all Millennials stated their cell phone is vital to their lives. This response rate is not surprising. There is almost nothing a cell phone cannot do when it comes to communication. While it does not produce a handwritten letter, you can IM, text, or write e-mails on a cell phone now. And let's not forget that you can talk on a cell phone too.

The cell phone is the key player in the ever-changing world of communication. Communication is changing even within the Millennial Generation. There is a difference in communication methods between the older and younger Millennials.

Based on the question at the beginning of this section, we were able to break down responses based on age. To keep it simple, we divided the Millennials that we interviewed in half by age. The younger group is made up of those eighteen to twenty-three years of age. The older group is twenty-four to thirty years of age. Let's look at the communication difference between the two groups:

Younger Millennials
- Phone (34 percent)
- Text (47 percent)
- E-mail (10 percent)
- IM (8 percent)

Older Millennials
- Phone (43 percent)
- Text (28 percent)
- E-mail (20 percent)
- IM (7 percent)

We have two main observations from this age comparison. The first observation is the difference in texting. Younger Millennials use texting as a primary form of communication almost 20 percentage points more than older Millennials. Texting was higher than phone use by 13 percentage points for the younger Millennials. Phone use was 15 percentage points higher than texting for the older Millennials. A communication shift from phone to texting is occurring even from within the Millennial Generation.

Our second observation is the number of primary communication methods. Younger Millennials appear to simplify the way they communicate. Older Millennials claim three different methods: phone, text, and e-mail. Younger Millennials claim two different methods: phone and text. There is a large drop-off from the second to the third communication method for the younger Millennials.

Social Media

We are hard pressed to find a straightforward, reasoned definition of social media. Probably one of the most accurate definitions we came across read something to the effect of "a million different definitions to a million different people." We decided to ask those who are avid users of social media, the Millennials, their impressions of social media.

"What does social media mean to you?" we asked Paul. He responded, "Social media is a way I can have interaction with my friends and family even if we are miles apart. The social aspect is obvious. Media refers to the method of communication. If no information is being transmitted, it fails to be media. In a way it's personal information transmitted to another person or people."

Impressed by Paul's insight into social media, we asked him to elaborate. Paul began, "I believe social media needs to be electronic. I think anything in a print format is not fast enough to keep pace with my social life."

Paul's comments helped solidify much of our thinking about social media. He energized us for one last interview. We hoped to glean just a little more insight about the Millennials' approach to social media. In our last interview we had a chance to speak with Lee. We posed the same statement to him, "Tell us what social media means to you." Lee paused for a moment. His thoughts were formulating. He looked at us and said, "Facebook." With no disagreement on our part, we called it a day.

Social media by popularity. We define *social media* as instantaneous social communication where a transfer of information takes place with two or more people. A lot of communication venues fit our definition. So we asked the Millennials to pinpoint which social media avenues they use the most. Here are the Millennials' top social media sites:

- Facebook (73 percent)
- MySpace (49 percent)
- Reading Blogs (30 percent)
- Twitter (18 percent)
- Writing Blogs (13 percent)
- LinkedIn (6 percent)

It is little surprise that Facebook ranks at the top. Facebook was initially started by a Millennial for Millennials. It now reaches around the world with millions of daily users. MySpace as the second choice of social media sites is not surprising either. MySpace was the main social media site for several years beginning around 2006. But in 2008 Facebook surpassed MySpace in popularity.

The Millennials ranked LinkedIn as the least used social media site. LinkedIn is mainly used for business purposes. The site tries to create a network of people in order to help find jobs or create business opportunities. Its place in the social realm is limited.

Blogs continue to hang in the balance of social media. Those who use blogs tend to be faithful in their blogging endeavors. Blogs require more time and energy than other social media avenues. For that reason blogs typically do not draw in the large numbers like other social media avenues.

Twitter is the most recent social media site. Those who "tweet" are limited to statements containing no more than 140 characters. Brevity is a must for all Twitter users. Twitter has not reached the user levels like those of Facebook and MySpace. But Twitter is no small site. Currently there are more than seventy-five million people registered on Twitter. Interestingly Twitter is not yet drawing Millennial users into the micro-blogging world. Only one out of five Millennials uses Twitter.

Social media by education. Twitter and the Millennials have not found the connection like other social media sites. The other social media sites are not without their challenges in reaching all the Millennials. To give you an idea of the varying usage of social media, we decided to break down social media usage by education level.

Two key components surfaced in this analysis. First, Facebook is the clear choice for Millennials. At no point did any other social media site surpass Facebook. Second, the higher the education of a respondent, the more likelihood he or she will use a social media site. The previous statement has one exception though. Those with less education were more likely to use MySpace.

In addition to the two key components, those who have graduate degrees are more involved with social media than others. Almost one out of two graduate-level Millennials read blogs. More than 80 percent of graduate-level Millennials use Facebook. And one out of four graduate-level Millennials use LinkedIn. Millennials with graduate degrees are the most active social media users of the Millennial Generation.

With so many active social media users, one may forget that not all Millennials are involved with social media. More than 150 out of the twelve hundred interviewed Millennials said they did not use Facebook, MySpace, Twitter, LinkedIn, or blogs. That equals 13 percent of the Millennial Generation. For a generation so heavily involved in technology, this percentage may seem high. Some Millennials are making a conscious decision not to use social media.

Computer use. The Millennials are heavily involved with social media. As Thom and Jess researched further on what this meant for the Millennials, the question arose about how much time the Millennials are spending on the computer. Social media is accessed through different technologies, but the most pervasive is a computer. So we decided to ask how much time during the week the Millennials spend on a computer for both work and personal use.

Let's start with time spent on a computer for work. Not assuming that every Millennial uses a computer for work, we first asked how many Millennials use a work computer. Eighty-three percent responded that they use a computer for work. Of those 83 percent, the average number of hours spent per week on a work computer is seventeen hours. For those who enjoy boring statistics, the median number of hours is ten.

One out of five Millennials use their work computer for forty or more hours per week. Not only is this the largest amount of hours but also the largest percentage of computer use. Sixteen percent use a work computer for one to four hours per week. These 16 percent represent the fewest amounts of hours and the second largest percentage of work computer use.

When we looked at the subgroups of which Millennials spent more time, five subgroups had dramatically higher usage than their counterparts. We discovered that Millennial women use the computer for work more than men; older Millennials more than younger; higher-income Millennials more than lower income, Asian Millennials more than Whites, African-Americans, or Hispanics; and higher-educated Millennials more than lower educated.

Almost every Millennial reported time spent on a computer for personal use. The responses varied from less than five hours per week to more than thirty hours per week. The largest number of Millennials stated they spend ten to fourteen hours a week on a personal computer. This group represented one-fourth of all Millennials. The average amount of time on a personal computer is seventeen hours.

These numbers may be making your head spin. Yeah, we can get carried away with all these statistics. To help put all of these numbers in perspective, let's see how these percentages and numbers fit into a normal week. There are 168 hours in a week. We will assume that typical Millennials sleep eight hours per night. That equals fifty-six hours of sleep per week. That leaves 112 waking hours per week.

The average Millennial spends seventeen hours per week on a computer for work. The average Millennial also spends seventeen hours per week on a computer for personal use. That totals thirty-four hours per week on a computer. Thus average Millennials spends 30 percent of their time awake on a computer. *That means roughly one-third of Millennials' waking lives are spent on a computer.*

Computers are becoming more and more a part of their daily lives. The Millennials work, play, and socialize through the computer. For many it's their connection to the world. Media, especially social media, influences the Millennial Generation. So let's see just how much.

Influencing the Millennials

Nothing is more powerful and influential than the Millennials' parents. Friends and extended family are there for secondary support. The Millennials still look to other sources beyond these close relationships. They have connections to many positive, outside sources at their fingertips.

Looking beyond friends and family, where do the Millennials find influence? Music ranked as the most influential media source. Sixty-one percent of the Millennial Generation stated that music was a positive influence on their lives. Thom spoke about his enjoyment of 1960s music. Growing up, his ability to listen to the music he wanted was mostly in the hands of the radio disc jockey. Millennials find their influential music at the touch of a button. They can download a song in an instant. Millennials are in complete control of what they listen to and when they listen to it.

Over half of the Millennials find the Internet a positive influence. Fifty-five percent said that they find influence on Web sites and blogs. Just like music, information is a click away. If the Millennials do not like the way music or the Internet is influencing them, they have another option. One more push of a button will turn on the television. Thirty-two percent of the Millennials found television as a positive source of influence.

Most generations can find positive influence from these same sources. What is fascinating are the sources the Millennials are not turning to as influencers. Music, Internet, and television each outranked religious beliefs, a spouse, and a boss in terms of influence. Music is more influential than religious beliefs by three percentage points. The Internet is more influential than a spouse by 30 percentage points. And television is more influential than a boss by 11 percentage points.

It is getting harder for traditional sources of influence to compete with the media. The Millennials are constantly connected to multiple sources of influence. Information is processed in rapid movements. By the time a husband can sit down and talk to his wife about an important decision, he has already read multiple online sources and formulated an opinion.

Millennial husbands and wives are not the only ones of their generation to adapt to the influence of media. The Millennial Generation can easily stay connected with anyone at anytime. Privacy has been redefined. Older generations have never seen this type of connectivity. The Boomers growing up only had to take the home phone off the hook in order to disconnect with the world. Media has influenced the Millennials to put a lot of their lives on public display.

Media has caused attention spans to decrease dramatically. The Millennial Generation is used to short bursts of information. Twitter restricts any comment to 140 characters. Brevity is a must for the Millennials. Acronyms and abbreviations are a part of the Millennial language.

The Millennial Generation is accustomed to instant information. Media produces instantaneous results. There is no waiting, especially in communication. E-mails usually receive a response within half a day. Facebook messages will be answered within a couple of hours. Text messages are returned within thirty minutes, although most respond within the first few minutes.

Media has brought both new safety features and safety concerns to the Millennials. Millennials in need of immediate assistance simply need to pick up their cell phone and call for help. GPS locations can be obtained from a cell phone. A person can be located within minutes. At the same time text messaging while driving is considered to be more dangerous than driving while intoxicated. Millennials also use instant communication for inappropriate and unethical purposes. Courts and lawyers are dealing with new crimes never committed before because of media.

Media is influential. While many good results have come from media, unfortunately bad consequences have surfaced as well. The Millennials will continue to have access to the latest forms of media. How that media influences them is their choice.

An Empowered Generation

Media is powerful. Social media is more powerful. This young American generation is empowered by media. The impact Millennials have already made through media and social media is undeniable. The grassroots movements that take place in the social-media world are amazing.

Millennials that disagree with the practices or products of a company can stage a boycott that can disrupt multimillion-dollar industries. It takes just one group or event on Facebook to cause CEOs to shake their heads in wonder.

The Millennial Generation understands their influence. When an issue is big enough to rally around, they will make their impact known. In 2008 the Millennials wanted change. They found a presidential candidate who offered change. A connection was established on YouTube, Facebook, and Twitter that helped elect Barack Obama as president of the United States.

It is not just the big influence that makes media powerful. It is the little influence as well. Millennials are finding new friends, business partners, and spouses via social media. Business or dating prospects are no longer limited to the nearest town. The world we live on is indeed flat and small.

The Millennials are keen to this new world. They understand the influence media has on them. They also understand the influence media allows them to have. Their voice can be heard. And they are using it.

Media will continue to change. But the way Millennials use it will not. Technology will continue to advance, and Millennials will quickly adapt. A new world of communication is now established, and Millennials are using it. Social media is the most powerful form of media; the Millennials feel empowered. The Millennial Generation is America's largest generation, and they well may be America's most powerful generation as well.

CHAPTER 9

The Millennials and Money

She knew that she had to walk through those double doors. She absolutely did not want to go.

Maria sat looking at the reflection of her car in the bank doors. She recalled her thoughts for us, "I will walk in as soon as this song is over." In the meantime she decided to take one more look over her bank statement.

We asked Maria to explain to us exactly what happened with her financial situation. "I don't know where I went wrong," she stated. "I knew the money in my account was getting low, but I never imagined I was overdrawn. It was during finals week, so I was not paying attention like I normally do."

Maria continued with her story, "When I finally looked at my account balance online, I was shocked! I had completely forgotten about the twenty-five-dollar check I wrote to the bookstore. It wasn't much, but it was enough for me to overdraw my checking account."

We decided to ask a little more about her financial situation, "Feel free to decline to answer this question, but did you have other money to cover the amount of the check?"

"I did!" Maria said emphatically. "My parents always taught me the importance of saving. I had plenty of money in my savings to cover the amount of the check."

"Now that you mentioned your parents, were they involved at any point during this time?" we asked.

Maria slowly began to grin. "Yeah, they were," she stated as if she knew we were going to ask that question. "When my account became overdrawn, I saw charges from the bank. I had no idea what they were, so I called my mom. She explained to me that every time my account goes into the negative, they charge me a fee. The whole thing still confuses me. You would think if I had enough money, then the bank would not charge me," she said.

"Now that we have the background, will you take us back to your story? You were sitting in your car about to go inside the bank," we asked.

Maria began, "My mom mentioned to me that since this was my first time overdrawing my account, the bank might help me out with the fees. She told me that I just needed to go and tell them my situation."

"I was embarrassed, but I knew I had to straighten out the mess I had made," she said.

Maria continued, "So I walked in [the bank]. One of the tellers brought me to a customer service representative who tried to explain the difference between insufficient and unavailable funds. I remember the words but still do not remember what they mean.

"What I do remember is that the man gave me a refund on one of the charges. He also linked my accounts together so it won't overdraw again. It was nice of him to do that," Maria stated. She concluded her story by saying, "He also talked to me about other accounts instead of my savings. At that point I could not think about other accounts. Two is more than enough for me."

The story Maria told us about her understanding of financial matters provided the perfect example of how most of the Millennials feel about finances. Jess gave his insight into the Millennials and money in chapter 2 when he stated the Millennials are financially confused.

Millennials are indeed confused, and their age plays a large role in their confusion. The confusion they may feel regarding money, however, is not due to a lack of interest in the topic. This generation is deliberate and focused, and we will follow up with their focus a little bit later. First, let's begin our look into Millennials and money by understanding exactly how their age is important to the way they handle and understand finances.

Money and Age

The Millennial Generation is young. In fact, the youngest member of the Millennials is ten years old at the time of the writing of this book. In terms of education, the youngest member is finishing fourth grade. The oldest member of the Millennials was thirty years old at the time of our study. As a reminder, our study focused only on older Millennials, those born between 1980 and 1991.

Let's compare the Millennial Generation to the generation that has a lot of Millennial children, the Boomers. The oldest Baby Boomer is currently sixty-five years old. The youngest Baby Boomer is forty-seven years old. The Baby Boomers are starting to retire. They are beginning to collect Social Security. They are leaving the workforce.

Millennials have just begun to think about retirement. Millennials are in the beginning stages of entering the workplace. Most Millennials have not even started to pay into Social Security. These two generations are entering opposite phases of life.

The age difference between these two generations is significant. Even a comparison with Generation X would prove to be a stark contrast, but we will keep the comparison to just one generation. Here is how the Millennials and Boomers compare in terms of age: The median age of the Baby Boomers is fifty-five. The median age of the Millennials is twenty. The comparison of median age differences leaves a thirty-five-year gap. The life experience of a fifty-five-year-old as compared to a twenty-year-old is different. While these numbers might be more information than you desired to know, they illustrate this point: The Millennials are a young generation.

The answers these respondents gave showed that the Millennials are thinking about financial issues. This generation thinks about savings. They think about retirement. They think about budgets.

The Millennials are gaining valuable experience when it comes to financial matters. Any naivete they have is quickly offset by their ability to locate and decipher information. This generation knows how to find the most recent and accurate data. Most young people in previous generations likely were not as focused on financial matters.

The initial responses Millennials provided us about money are fascinating. As this generation accumulates more life experience and knowledge, their responses are likely to change, though. But the trends and attitudes Millennials already display are intriguing. Let's take a quick look at one fascinating aspect of Millennials and money.

Eighty-three percent of Millennials said that having a high income is important to them. This statistic by itself does not sound any alarms. Having a high income is the American way, right? Let's not forget who we are talking about though. The Millennials believe they can make an impact for the future. It goes beyond belief as well; Millennials feel it is their responsibility to make an impact for the future.

Millennials do want to make money. They do want high incomes. But this generation also has a desire to serve society.

They want to use their time and efforts in order to make a difference. According to the Millennials, the two aspirations are not mutually exclusive.

While the Millennials' attitude toward financial matters is fascinating, it is also confusing. This generation wants to accomplish it all. As more Millennials enter the workplace, their confusion will move toward greater clarity. As they learn that time becomes more limited, Millennials will fine-tune their focus on what is important to them.

The overall financial picture of the Millennials is still hazy, but Millennials remain clear on many financial matters. Our research covered numerous issues involving money, and we were able to gain valuable insights into the minds of the Millennials.

What We Learned about the Millennials and Money

Our survey has a disproportionate number of questions related to financial matters. In return, the Millennials gave us numerous and multifaceted answers. While the information gathered is enough to produce another book, we chose to present the data that most fully represents the Millennials. The following sections include a lot of numbers and statistics. For those who may find numerical data uninteresting, each section will also include a summary of the data. So let's take a look at what we learned about the Millennials and money.

Are the Millennials in good hands? We began our financial section of the survey with questions about insurance. Specifically we were interested in finding out if the Millennials were comfortable with their coverage. Did they feel their current policies were sufficient? We asked about health insurance, home insurance, life insurance, and automotive insurance.

Our respondents were asked to rate their level of agreement with the following statement, "I have enough automotive insurance for my needs or my family's needs." Seventy-nine percent of Millennials agree they are properly covered for their automotive needs. Roughly one out of five Millennials believes he or she needs more automotive coverage.

The percentage of Millennials dropped when asked about proper insurance coverage on their home. Sixty percent of Millennials agreed that they have enough home insurance for their needs or their family's needs. The answer was virtually the same when asked about medical insurance. Fifty-eight percent agreed that they have enough medical insurance for their needs or their family's needs.

Even fewer Millennials seemed comfortable with their current level of life insurance. When asked to agree or disagree with the following statement, "I have enough life insurance for my needs or my family's needs," the Millennials were split. Only 51 percent of Millennials believe they have enough life insurance.

Okay, enough of this boring data about insurance. The bottom line is that the Millennial Generation believes they are underinsured. Typically, insurance rates and costs are lower with the younger population. While car rates are higher for younger drivers, the vehicles insured will usually have less value. The same applies to homes, as Millennials' homes are going to be typically of lower value than those in older generations. Life insurance costs less for younger people. Medical coverage becomes more costly during later years when more health problems arise.

Insurance should, therefore, be more affordable now rather than later. While income levels are lower now than they will be, Millennials are still finding it difficult to find sufficient insurance coverage while costs are low.

Save it or give it? Monthly income should be greater than monthly expenses. Well, at least that is the goal for every person or family who has a personal budget. When this goal is met, there is a surplus of money. For most families, that money is put into a savings vehicle. A lot of families also decide to give some of that money away. We asked the Millennials just how much they are saving and giving.

We asked a wide range of questions about the savings habits of Millennials. We asked questions about retirement, emergency funds, and the ease or difficulty of saving. We wanted to know what the Millennials are doing with their money. We will look in depth at the issue of this generation's savings habits later in this chapter.

So what about the Millennials who choose to give their money away? This question was asked of the twelve hundred Millennials, "In the past twelve months, has your household given any money or financial support to religious, charitable, or nonprofit organizations?" Six out of ten Millennials responded that they had financially supported a nonprofit organization.

Those Millennials who give money to a charitable cause have some common traits. Those with higher incomes are more likely to donate their money. Those with higher education are more likely to provide charitable giving. And those who are born again Christians and/or Evangelicals are also more likely to donate a portion of their income.

Regardless of who is giving, the fact remains that 60 percent of Millennials are giving their money to a charity, religious organization, or nonprofit group. This discovery may prove to be one of our more surprising insights about this generation. What you do with your money is a significant indicator of what you truly believe. The Millennial Generation is making a statement early in their years that they are choosing to give. They are looking beyond self to others.

3. **The other questions.** In addition to understanding the Millennials' insurance needs and their saving and giving habits, we sought to see the bigger financial picture. While these issues will be further addressed later in this chapter, let's take a quick look at the topics.

The Millennials were asked how much they expect from the government for both health care and retirement. We asked the Millennials to open up about their current financial situation. We looked at income levels for the Millennials. We asked how many Millennials were saving a portion of their income. We also asked how many Millennials were saving and planning specifically for retirement.

We wanted to know which financial concepts are foreign to Millennials and which concepts seem to make sense to them.

We asked questions concerning budgeting and personal financial plans. So much of this generation's attitudes toward money is formative for how they view the world now and later. We learned much about their worldview just by listening to them talk about money. One key insight, for example, is their view of the role of government in their financial matters.

The Millennials' Big Brother

"Who is FICA, and what are they doing with my money?" asked Wes, one of my (Jess') coworkers. The way Wes phrased his question I knew he already had an answer. Wes and I just finished our sophomore year of high school. We both had begun to work at a local fast-food restaurant inside one of Louisville's malls. It was our first job, and we were finally gaining some work experience.

I recall answering his question with a simplistic response, "It's the government. And I have no idea what they are doing with our money." Wes' attempted humor left me with a desire to understand more about where a portion of my paycheck was going every two weeks. I told Wes, "I'll find out though." That night I decided to do some in-depth research. I was going to ask my parents.

"Social Security or FICA is the government's way of making you put money aside for retirement," my dad told me. "They save the money for you and give you a monthly check when you retire. I want you to understand that it will not be enough money to maintain a good standard of living. What that means is, the money you receive from the government will not allow you to live comfortably. You need other income when you retire."

My dad continued, "You really need to have your own retirement plan. Social Security is good to supplement your own plan. But the current Social Security plan appears to be losing money. You will continue to pay into the plan but will receive a lot less or maybe nothing at all when you retire."

I have to admit I listened to Dad this time. From that point forward I began paying attention to my payroll deductions. While my paycheck's tax deduction description has changed over the years from FICA to SS to OASDI, I understand the government's aim to provide retirement benefits to retirees and those with disabilities.

The Millennial Generation also understands the government's goal to provide supplemental retirement. The Millennials have seen the deduction for Social Security from every one of their paychecks. But their awareness also leads to expectations. The Millennials like what Big Brother is doing. But they want Big Brother to give back to them. In fact, they expect a full return from the government.

We asked the Millennials to respond to the following statement, "It should be the government's responsibility to provide me with an adequate retirement." Sixty-two percent of Millennials agreed with this statement! Millennials do not seem bothered by the information about the precarious state of government-provided retirement. They have seen numerous articles on the Internet about the demise of Social Security. Roughly two out of three Millennials do not seem to care about the current government retirement situation. They seem to have an attitude of "It just better be fixed by the time I retire."

Millennials are not looking to Big Brother for just retirement but also for health coverage. We asked Millennials the same question about health coverage and to respond to the following statement, "It should be the government's responsibility to provide me with adequate health insurance or coverage." Sixty-six percent of Millennials stated they agreed with the statement.

Along with other generations, Millennials are paying into the government health-care system. They expect a good return on their money.

We found some surprises among the different subgroups on this issue. A natural presumption is that those with lower income levels may have higher expectations of government aid. This is not the case with the Millennial Generation. Regardless of income level, the expectation was almost the same that the government will take responsibility for retirement and health care.

The expectation for help from the government comes from all subgroups of Millennials. As the Millennial Generation ages, these expectations might well change. It will be fascinating to see what direction America's largest generation takes.

A Surprising Find

"How many years has it been since you graduated college?" we asked Libby.

"I just reached the four-year mark. It is amazing how quickly the time has gone by. It seems like it was last year that I graduated high school," she responded.

"You mentioned you majored in communications. Why did you choose this major?"

Libby answered, "I always heard people in the field talk about how good the pay is and how great the benefits are. Plus, I don't want to spend a lot of time behind a desk. I like to be out meeting people. It just fits me."

We continued the conversation by asking, "So would it be safe to say that your current career choice is mainly based on financial reasons?"

Libby was quick to reply, "Yes, but do not get me wrong here. I also chose the profession because of the flexibility. I love being able to take time to be with my family or to have time to myself."

"You just mentioned that you want to be able to spend time with family. Are there other relationships in your life that you desire this with as well?" we asked.

"Definitely," Libby said. "My boyfriend and I have been together for about two years now. We are both dedicated to each other, but we don't plan to get married for a couple more years. Right now, we are both focusing on our careers. Although marriage and kids are on the horizon, it just is not in the picture right now."

Libby's conversation with us was surprising at the time. Almost all of the other participants in the study focused on family issues before they mentioned any work-related or financial matters. Although Libby mentioned family, it was an afterthought to her career. Of course Libby graduated from college, and that timing undoubtedly affected her responses to us.

When the research was finished and compiled, Libby's conversation began to make more sense. When asked of the Millennials, 83 percent agreed that having a high income is important to them.

Think back to previous chapters. Millennials are focused on family. It is their first priority. Millennials are not workaholics. They must have balance between their work and personal life. Millennials are focused on making an impact on the future. Societal contribution is important to the Millennial Generation.

So how does having a high income fit into the Millennials' plans? Maybe our conversation with Libby provides a glimpse into how this might play out. She desired to have a career in place before she began a family. Maybe she will give back to society in her later years.

Maybe the Millennial Generation will find a way to achieve both their idealistic ambitions and financial success. For right now, there seems to be some confusion in the Millennial Generation. Their confusion is the greatest when it comes to financial matters.

Understanding the Confusion

"The whole thing still confuses me," Maria told us during her story at the beginning of this chapter. She had learned that what sometimes is thought of as a simple process can turn into a complex matter. She admitted that even after someone explained to her how she accrued fees, she still remained confused. At the time we were unable to tell her the following statement, but we can now: "Maria, you are not alone."

We asked the Millennials outright if financial matters confused them. Participants were asked to state if they agree or disagree with the following statement: "Financial matters tend to confuse me." Thirty-eight percent of Millennials agreed that financial matters confuse them. Frankly, such confession is unusual. Roughly two out of every five Millennials are seeking clarity on how to manage their money properly.

We can go back just a few pages in this chapter to see where some of the confusion begins. Remember that Millennials desire a high income. In fact, 83 percent of the Millennial Generation wants a high income. At the same time approximately two-thirds of Millennials believe that the government should provide retirement and health-care benefits. This is unusual since those with high incomes usually have no need for government assistance.

Career success is near the top of the Millennial agenda. In addition to success, Millennials also have a desire to achieve wealth. More than eight out of ten respondents stated that they have a goal of achieving at least modest wealth. The connection between career success and modest wealth is easy to understand. But not all the issues related to Millennials' view of finances was that easy to comprehend.

As a Millennial, I (Jess) believe that a lot of confusion comes from the complex financial system that is currently in place.

It takes a lot of work and a lot of time to determine the right way to manage money. While having many options may seem positive, it begins to get confusing when this generation tries to determine which option is best. Financial complexity definitely leads to confusion for these young adults. The complexity likely contributes to their lack of trust on many financial matters.

The Millennials' distrust of finances in general has not been helped by the worst economic downturn since the Depression, commonly called the Great Recession. We remind you at the risk of redundancy that this generation, like others, has experienced a number of formative events. Many Millennials view life from a financial perspective through the lens of the Great Recession.

Take a look at what the Millennials experienced so far. Their parents' homes, the primary asset for most families, have fallen in value, some dramatically. Some Millennials' parents have even left their homes with a mortgage exceeding the value of the house. Investment accounts, such as IRAs and 401(k)s, have tanked. Parents of Millennials have returned to work or taken on second jobs. Unemployment rates have been at record highs. Millennials thought a college education would land them a good-paying job. Instead many Millennials find themselves filling the first entry-level position that becomes available.

Homes, cars, jobs, and savings have historically been a part of the middle-class American dream. Millennials are watching older generations, especially the Boomers, lose possessions that were once taken for granted. The Millennials were taught by their parents to spend wisely, to buy a home when possible, to save for retirement, and to expect good jobs to be available. But that world came crashing down in the Great Recession. It's easy to see why the Millennials are confused.

We don't know the lasting effects of the financial confusion on the Millennial Generation. We can hope the Millennials will learn from the mistakes they are witnessing. While the future is unknown, the Millennials may indeed be learning valuable lessons. They are already showing signs of moving in a positive financial direction. Let's look at some reasons to hope that the largest generation in America's history may be responsible stewards of their finances.

Saving for the Future

The Bureau of Economic Analysis, a division of the U.S. Department of Commerce, monitors the personal savings rate of the United States. Historically America has been a country of people who save. The Bureau provides interesting insights about American savings habits from 1959 until 2010. Americans, we learn, have traditionally saved upwards of 7 and 8 percent in any given month.

In the early 1990s our habits changed, and savings have consistently declined ever since. Savings rates declined rapidly from the last decade of the millennium to around 2005. The savings rate actually moved below 1 percent to a negative savings rate. Simply stated, Americans began to spend more money than they were making. In recent years the personal saving rate began trending upward. The Great Recession had its impact. Americans were rethinking their spending and saving habits.

How does the Millennials' view of money fit into these savings trends? We asked the Millennials how easy it is for them to save money. Forty-eight percent of the generation finds it easy to save money. This number is not only high for the Millennials, but it is high for any generation. If their attitude about savings continues, we will once again be a nation that saves. Indeed, saving money appears to be a high financial priority for this generation.

Okay, one out of two Millennials say saving money is easy. But how much are the Millennials really saving? During our conversations Clayton told us about his thought process regarding saving money.

"I went four and a half months without a job," Clayton began. "I worked with a communication firm for just over three years. One day the company president announced they were restructuring a couple of the company's divisions. Long story short, that meant I was let go. I understand why they did it, but I was left without any income. My wife was still working, but it really made me start to think. What if she lost her job too?"

We asked Clayton, "How did this impact your savings habits?"

Clayton responded, "It changed them for the better. I was able to find a new job in broadcasting. In fact, it was a large enough pay increase in salary that my wife now works part-time. We started saving until we knew that we would have enough money to live on for five months if neither of us had a job."

Clayton saved enough money for five months of living expenses. How much have other Millennials saved? We asked how many Millennials had enough savings to cover six months of living expenses. Twenty-eight percent of Millennials responded positively to this question. Over one out of four Millennials is able to go without income for six months. This statistic is extremely encouraging for a generation that has just begun to save. And it defies the pattern of many in older generations.

They are not only finding it easy to save but are saving relatively large amounts. The Millennial Generation is on track for long-term savings as well. We asked Millennials to agree or disagree with the following statement: "I am currently saving money for retirement." Thirty-seven percent of them are saving for retirement.

Retirement experts emphasize the importance of saving early. The analogy of the snowball is often used to illustrate the power of saving early. The snowball starts off small and rolls slowly. As time passes, the snowball grows and rolls faster. It eventually becomes a force of its own. Millennials are beginning to start rolling their own snowballs. The benefits of their good stewardship may not be fully evident early on. However, if they continue their current savings patterns, Millennials will begin to see more and more progress in the area of retirement savings.

The Millennials' views on savings are encouraging. The financial trends for them are positive. They appear to understand the importance for saving for both the short-term and the long-term. As a consequence, many of the Millennials will not be burdened with excessive debt. The Millennials will have different spending habits from those of previous generations. The "I want it now" mentality of their predecessors, especially the Baby Boomers, may not be typical of the Millennials. This generation could well be the generation that turns back the financial clock to greater savings and more conservative spending.

A Renewed Focus on Budgeting

I (Thom) taught Jess a lot about money growing up. It was natural for me to instill principles about money in Jess, as finances were part of my upbringing. My dad was president of a small bank in the town where I grew up in Alabama. As soon as I reached my teenage years, my dad put me behind the teller line in his bank. Once I gained a couple years of experience, my dad taught me how to underwrite loans. While this is not the typical upbringing for a young teenager, the experience taught me much about managing money.

While I could not give my three boys the experience my father gave me (banking regulations have changed slightly since then), I tried to teach them as much as I could. It was important that they knew the basics of finance. I started a savings account for each son right after each birth. When they met the age requirements, they opened a joint checking account with my wife and me. They each received a credit card while they were in high school.

Throughout each step I showed my sons how to balance their savings, reconcile their checkbooks, and pay their credit card bills on time. While they did not have a steady source of income, I taught them to plan for purchases. It was my way to teach them to budget. I guess what I taught them stayed with them. Each of my three sons majored in finance during college, and each has held or currently holds a job in the finance field.

I (Jess) did follow in my grandfather, father, and brothers' footsteps. It was hard to deviate from such a well-worn path. Although the decision to major in finance during college was my own, my family history played a role in my decision. More importantly, my dad's teachings stayed with me. His lessons are invaluable. They laid a financial foundation that will carry my wife and me through the rest of our lives.

The key to my dad's financial lessons was simple. Save, save, and save. As I slowly transitioned to financial independence, it became hard to save, save, and save. Then budgeting became a vital part of my personal finances. My wife and I have tried multiple budgeting methods. We started with traditional budget books. We then moved to a computer program. We tried a cash envelope system. Our fourth and final move is to an Internet-based automatic budget. While there is ample room for improvement, we are still budgeting. Even amid all the changes in method, the option to stop budgeting never arose.

Jess' approach to budgeting matches the Millennials' view toward budgeting. Eighty-four percent of Millennials view budgeting as important. This is an incredibly high number. Millennials are clearly focused on their finances. This generation wants to know where and how they are spending their money.

The Millennials also want control of their money. The financial industry is appealing to this generation and others about regaining control of personal finances. Automated payments and direct deposit eliminate the chances of missed payments and lost checks. Online viewing of checking and savings account is popular. The ability to transfer money in an instant is another way of providing control to personal finances.

The Millennials' skepticism of the finance industry was indeed an outcome of the Great Recession. Budgeting is a means by which the Millennial Generation will begin to regain trust and control of their personal finances. Remember, 84 percent of the Millennials believe budgeting is important. The Millennials appear to have a financial plan. And that is exactly what we asked the Millennials next.

A Plan for the Future

Investment guidance. Financial review. Retirement planning. Portfolio analysis. And the list could keep going.

Whichever set of words is used, the meaning is often the same. Those in the financial industry want to help clients develop a plan to meet their goals. A road map traces an individual's current financial status to where he or she desires to be in the future. Stops along the way may include putting children through college, a second home, a vacation home, the start of a new business, or early retirement.

Financial planning is a buzzword in the finance field. The recent rise of interest in financial planning led to the creation of a certification for financial planning. Without giving too much of a history lesson, the certification for a financial planner took a major step in the mid-1980s by the creation of a nonprofit certifying board. In the mid-1990s, this board became the certifying body for Certified Financial Planners (CFP). The lesson is clear. People are seeking advice for financial planning more than ever before.

We asked the Millennials to tell us about their financial plans. The responses to our interviews varied, but they did have common features. We asked them to respond to the follow statement: "I have a financial plan for the future." Here are some of their responses:

- "Yes. I have a five-, ten-, and fifteen-year plan. Although the plans do include other life goals."
- "Kind of. I have some goals I want to achieve, and that includes having enough money to retire when I am sixty-five."
- "I do, but I have never written them down or formalized them."
- "Not really. All I want to do is finish school without too much debt."
- "Absolutely. My wife and kids are so important to me that I want to make sure they are taken care of no matter what."

Our research showed that almost two-thirds of Millennials have a financial plan for the future. This strong response is yet another encouraging sign about this generation and money. The Millennials continue to surprise us with their responses, surprises that paint a positive financial picture for the future.

Confused but Trying Hard

The Millennials told us both directly and indirectly that they are confused when it comes to financial matters. Confusion fueled by a faltering economy, a complex financial system, and financial distrust will take time to return to a sense of normalcy. The Millennials are trying hard to make sense of what they are experiencing and have experienced.

Millennials are saving in relatively unprecedented amounts for such a young generation. This generation understands the need for both a short-term and long-term savings plan. They also understand it is not too early to start funding retirement accounts. The Millennials are not taking these financial steps blindly either. They have a financial plan.

You have heard us use words such as *positive* or *encouraging* throughout this chapter. The Millennials give us reason to view their financial activities from this perspective. Their actions put them on a track that will not allow a repeat of the mistakes they witness. Time will tell just how much their current financial decisions will reap in the years to come.

For now, the Millennials continue to navigate a financial world that is complex and confusing. This is not the only world that they currently navigate, though. The Millennial Generation walks through a spiritual world that is unlike any other generation. We will uncover their strange religious world in the next chapter.

CHAPTER 10

Their Strange Religious World

Brandon was born in the same month as Jess, April 1985. Only a few days separate their birth moments. Early in this book you heard from Jess about his spiritual beliefs. He is a Christian. He is a born-again Christian. He is an Evangelical, born-again Christian. We'll define those terms shortly; not everyone has the same meaning attached to each of them.

Only a minority of the Millennials holds Jess' beliefs. But there is no majority spiritual position in the entire generation. To the contrary, many have such a hodgepodge of beliefs that it's difficult to give them meaningful labels.

Back to Brandon. His belief system is a minority position as well. In fact we're not sure we could identify any of the other 1,199 respondents who held the same beliefs as Brandon. But then we listened to a lot of Millennials who had a unique religious system.

When we asked Brandon if he was a Christian, he responded quickly, "Sure I am." We knew better than to accept that response at face value, so we asked him to articulate his Christian beliefs.

"Well, most Americans are Christians, and so I guess I am too," he began. "I think my parents are Christians, but I've never really asked them. I have a pretty good feel for Jesus. I'm sure he was a good man like most religious leaders. He and Billy Graham would be pretty high on the list."

We questioned him about an afterlife. Again the response was candid and unique. "First of all," he said emphatically, "no one can really have a clue what happens when we die. I guess there is enough evidence to indicate that somehow we live on, but I'm not sure what that will look like. I kind of believe that there might be several possibilities. Some people may decide to come back as someone else, you know, reincarnation. Others may just want to retire and go to some good place in the afterlife. Maybe some have some scores to settle, so they have to deal with some folks before they move on. That's probably where we get our ghosts."

And then when we asked him if there was any authoritative source for spiritual beliefs, Brandon admitted his uncertainty. "I really don't think we can say that any one person or any book is a real authority." He paused for a moment and then continued. "You really have to examine what people say and then decide. You could find some truth in the Bible and maybe the

Koran. But you could find it in other sources as well, like a book by Billy Graham."

Brandon liked Billy Graham.

Though Brandon has his own unique religious system, he did have two commonalities with his Millennial peers. First, a Millennial is more likely than not to have a syncretistic belief system. He or she tends to take portions of belief from various faiths and nonfaiths and blend them into a unique spiritual system. Second, a Millennial is likely to care less about religious or spiritual matters than his or her predecessor generations.

Look again, for example, at the top ten most important things in life for a Millennial. The way we asked the question in our research was open ended, so the respondents were free to craft their own answers.

What Is Really Important in Your Life?
1. Family (61 percent)
2. Friends (25 percent)
3. Education (17 percent)
4. Career/job (16 percent)
5. Spouse/partner (13 percent)
6. Spiritual matters (13 percent)
7. Finances (12 percent)
8. Happiness (12 percent)
9. Raising kids (11 percent)
10. Health (10 percent)

After we pressed Brandon a bit further on religious and spiritual matters, he became more transparent with his feelings. "Look guys, I know religion is important to a lot of people," he continued his thoughts. "But I'm not really one of those people who even thinks much about religion. I'm not against religions or religious people; it's just not who I am. I call myself a Christian because that's the label my family's had for generations. But I doubt that I'm even close to being like those people who attend church a lot. Religion is just really low on my list of priorities."

Brandon's belief system is not typical of his generation. There is no typical belief system among the Millennials. But Brandon's laissez-faire attitude about religious matters was common. "Spiritual matters" were sixth in importance to the members of this generation, and that priority was affirmed by only 13 percent of the respondents. Brandon's words expressed the overall sentiment well: "Religion is just really low on my list of priorities."

Understanding the Terms

Religious beliefs were one of the major categories for our research on the Millennials, but that category has the potential to be the most confusing. The problem is that different people define religious terms differently.

The term *Christian* was not defined. It was one of many religious systems that could be chosen by the Millennial. We therefore had a number of self-described Christians like Brandon who really did not hold to the historic tenets of orthodox Christianity. Using the broad and undefined term of Christian, 65 percent of the Millennials expressed it to be their religious preference.

A relatively few Millennials chose other religions. Judaism, Hindu, Muslim, Wiccan, and pagan were selected by 2 percent or less. But, surprisingly, atheism (God does not exist) was the religious preference of 6 percent. Agnosticism (uncertain or doubtful that God exists) was selected by 8 percent. And 14 percent had no preference at all.

Those three categories total 28 percent. Nearly three out of ten Millennials have moved completely away from certain beliefs in God. We plan to ask these same questions in future years to see if this is a trend in this generation.

Because the two of us are interested to see how our own belief system fares among the Millennials, we asked two further descriptive questions. We knew, as indicated above, that the number who affirmed Christianity as their preferred religion really did not give us insights into the number of Millennial Christians.

We therefore asked the respondents if they were "born-again Christians." This time we were more precise in our definition. We defined born-again Christians as those who have made a personal commitment to Jesus Christ and believe they will go to heaven because they have confessed their sins and accepted Christ as their Savior. Twenty percent affirmed this definition of their belief and experience.

We were even more precise when we attempted to discern how many of the Millennials are Evangelicals. Once again for reasons of full disclosure, we want to remind the reader that our beliefs are those of Evangelicals. It was our attempt to understand the proportion of this generation that holds to historical Christian beliefs.

As we surveyed the twelve hundred Millennials, we gave them a series of statements. In order to be categorized as an Evangelical, they had to be born-again Christians who also strongly:

- Agree the Bible is the accurate, written Word of God
- Agree they personally have the responsibility to tell others about their religious beliefs
- Agree their religious faith is important in their lives
- Agree God is all-knowing, all-powerful, and rules the universe today
- Agree salvation is available through grace alone
- Disagree Jesus committed sins while on Earth
- Disagree that Satan is not a living being but just a symbol of evil

Only 6 percent of Millennials could affirm the statements as written above. Obviously, the representation of true Christians in this generation is small. We cannot know with certainty the spiritual state of these young men and women. We can say, however, that as Christians we are concerned with what appears to be a low number.

We must be careful in making any conclusions. But, based on the 20 percent who could affirm the basic "born again" tenets, and based on the 6 percent who strongly agreed with the Evangelical statements, we would surmise that 10 to 15 percent of Millennials are true Christians. For consistency, we will stick with the 15 percent estimate.

Heaven Bound?

In light of their beliefs, it is fascinating to hear from this generation about their perceptions of their own eternal destinies. The most common response was that no one can know what will happen when they die (34 percent). Again, we must keep in mind the relative youth of these Millennials. Most were twentysomethings when we interviewed them. It is conceivable that weighty matters such as life after death are not at the forefront of the minds of this youthful generation.

More than one-fourth (26 percent), however, said they believe they will go to heaven when they die because they have accepted Christ as their Savior. Remember, 65 percent of this generation expressed a broadly Christian religious preference, but no more than 20 percent has a biblical understanding of Jesus and matters of salvation. Apparently some Millennials who are Christians in name only believe the label is sufficient to get them to heaven.

Almost one out of five Millennials think their works will get them to heaven. A few in this group explicitly identified obedience to the Ten Commandments as salvific.

The remainder of those surveyed have varied views of their eternal destinies. Five percent say they will be reincarnated. Four percent believe everyone goes to heaven, and 8 percent simply believe they will cease to exist. This generation is indeed a confused generation spiritually.

Beliefs and Behaviors

In Matthew 7:16–21 Jesus declared that His true followers could be recognized by both belief and actions. He described actions as "fruit." Look at His vivid descriptions:

> You'll recognize them by their fruit. Are grapes gathered from thornbushes or figs from thistles? In the same way, every good tree produces good fruit, but a bad tree produces bad fruit. A good tree can't produce bad fruit; neither can a bad tree produce good fruit. Every tree that doesn't produce good fruit is cut down and thrown into the fire. So you'll recognize them by their fruit. Not everyone who says to Me, 'Lord, Lord!' will enter the kingdom of heaven, but only the one who does the will of My Father in heaven.

Jesus' teaching was clear. Not all who claim Him as Lord will get to heaven. Only those who show the fruit of a true conversion will enter the kingdom of heaven.

With that in mind, we included "fruit inspection" questions in our research. Again, we realize that this approach is fallible as well, but it does give us even more insight into the spiritual realities of the Millennials.

Shall We Pray?

Despite the relative few Millennials who affirm basic Christian beliefs, exactly 50 percent of those we surveyed said they prayed once a week or more. On the other extreme, 38 percent indicated they prayed rarely or never.

Amanda was born in 1983. She is one of those rare Floridians who has lived in the state all of her life. In fact she has never moved from southwest Florida and is currently living in Sarasota. Unlike the majority of the Millennials in our study, Amanda can't trace a Christian lineage in her family, at least through her grandparents.

"As far as I know," Amanda began, "neither my parents nor my grandparents attended church or professed any kind of religious beliefs. I can count on one hand the number of times I've been inside a church, and I think all but one of those was for a wedding."

Amanda makes no pretense to be a Christian, even in name only. She has no antagonism toward Christians either. It's really not a part of her life. "There are a number of young adults just like me," she declares. "Religion has never been and probably never will be mixed up in our lives."

But we are curious. If she has no religious inclinations, why does she pray at least once a week? Is that not inconsistent with her beliefs? "I guess we all have a tendency to ask for help,"

Amanda explained. "Frankly, when I pray, I don't even know who or what I'm praying to. I'm not even sure there's anybody to pray to. But what if there is? I have nothing to lose and a lot to gain. Besides, praying is kind of therapeutic for me."

From our interviews we can make no conclusions about religious beliefs and those involved in prayer. When we asked the Millennials in our survey if they prayed with other people, the response, predictably, was lower. Still, given the religious inclinations of this generation, the fact that one out of four (24 percent) Millennials pray with others was surprising.

Going to Church?

We who have been studying the American church for some time know that each generation from the Boomers forward is less likely to attend church services. In the case of the Millennials, the trend continues. Nearly two-thirds (65 percent) of this generation rarely or never attend religious services. Our study used the more generic description "religious services" so that those who attend a service of non-Christian faith could respond. Still, most of the respondents specified Protestant or Roman Catholic services.

About one-fourth (24 percent) of the Millennials are active in church, attending at least once a week. If our assumption that 15 percent of the generation are Christians, that would mean that a number of Millennials would be true seekers. They are not Christians, but they are sufficiently interested in the faith to attend church at least once a week.

On the one hand, those of us who are Christians could have a number of reasons to be discouraged. Only a small portion of this generation is Christian. A number of them truly represent a post-Christian mind-set. Also, the Millennials who are active in church represent a dramatically smaller segment than previous generations.

On the other hand, those who are Christians demonstrate fervency about their faith. As we will discuss at the end of this chapter, the few may actually be more potent for Christianity than the many of previous generations. Hear the words of Melanie. She expresses this sentiment well.

"I am a Christian," she says frankly. "I have repented of my sins and place my faith in Jesus Christ. I have no doubt that I will go to heaven when I die." She pauses and gets her breath. "Look, I know that most of the people in my generation are not Christians. I was not raised in a Christian home, so I know that perspective."

Melanie then looked us right in the eyes. "And I know that being a Christian these days comes with a cost," she says with greater emphasis. "In some parts of the world, you can lose your life for being a Christian. What I'm trying to say is that I have counted the cost for my beliefs. I'm ready and willing to do whatever it takes to follow Jesus. I've seen too many cultural Christians in churches that don't have a clue. I'm not playing games. I'm serious, and I'm ready to take a stand for him no matter what the cost."

Churches that are serious about reaching this generation must become serious missional churches. Millennials like

Melanie don't have any patience with anything less than total commitment.

Time in the Bible

If the amount of time Millennials spend in the Bible is any indication of their Christian commitment, our estimates that 15 percent of the generational members are Christian may be close. We understand fully that some people read faith books of other religions only as an exercise of scholarship or curiosity. "I read the Bible almost every week," Adam told us. "But I sure wouldn't label me a Christian. I have only been in church a few times, and I don't come close to believing like most Christians. Still, I like reading the Bible. Parts of it are some of the most inspirational writings I've ever read."

Our survey of the Millennials actually included the breadth of so-called sacred writings. Even though we are Christians, we wanted to allow the respondents to tell us about any religious writings they read on a regular basis. We thus asked those surveyed to respond to two multiple-choice statements:

- You read the Bible, Torah, Koran, or other sacred writings (a) once a week or more; (b) less frequently; (c) rarely or never.
- You meet with other people to study the Bible, Torah, Koran, or other sacred writings (a) once a week or more; (b) less frequently; (c) rarely or never.

Though we offered as choices sacred writings beyond the Bible, almost all of our respondents indicated that they did not read the Torah, Koran, or other sacred writings in their responses to our follow-up interviews. We can surmise then that most of the Millennials were speaking of the Bible when they spoke of the frequency they read sacred writings. The responses were telling:

Frequency reading Bible (or other sacred writings):
- Once a week or more 21 percent
- Less frequently   12 percent
- Rarely or never   67 percent

Frequency meeting with others to study Bible (or other sacred writing):
- Once a week or more 15 percent
- Less frequently   6 percent
- Rarely or never   79 percent

Again, we are careful to correlate perfectly certain spiritual behaviors with Christian identity. A number of Millennials, as well as other generational members, told us they read the Bible, but they are not Christians. Conversely, we know that many Christians are not faithful in their time in the Bible. Both of us admit that we've had our own periods of inconsistency in our time studying the Bible individually or with others.

Still, the responses noted above would indicate that our thesis that 15 percent of Millennials are Christians would not be too far off, based on the behavioral pattern of Bible study indicated by the Millennials. Some of those who are in regular Bible study are likely devout Christians. Some are likely seeking answers for themselves about the Christian faith. And still others are clearly reading the Bible as a mere exercise of scholarship or curiosity.

What Then Do They Believe?

We asked the Millennials a series of questions from a Christian perspective. As Christian Evangelicals, we were curious to see how closely their beliefs corresponded to those of historic Christianity. In a quick summary the answer would be "not close." Indeed the responses were so diverse that discernment of any clear pattern was impossible.

On the surface, one of the surprise responses was to the statement: "You have made a personal commitment to Jesus Christ that is still important in your life today." One-third of the Millennials agreed strongly with the statement, and another 24 percent agreed somewhat. So 57 percent of the generation either agree or agree strongly about the personal importance of their commitment to Jesus Christ. How does such a strong affirmation make sense in light of our earlier hypothesis that 15 percent of Millennials are Christians? Or does it make sense in light of the response that showed that only 6 percent of the generation are Evangelical Christians? We think it does and can best be explained by our conversation with Brittany.

Brittany is twenty-five years old. She was raised in a single-parent home in upstate New York. She has no religious affiliation, nor did her mother who raised her. But she still has a positive view of Jesus Christ, at least Jesus as she understands him. Indeed, she was one of the 33 percent who agreed strongly that her commitment to Jesus Christ is still important in her life today.

"My commitment to Jesus is very real," Brittany began. "I see him as one of the pivotal figures of world history. He was one of the greatest men who ever lived." Our next question was waiting to be answered. Do you think Jesus was more than man? "No," she quickly responded. "He was a man just like Mohammed or Abraham Lincoln. But he was one of the greatest men who ever lived. I have followed his teachings, and I'm still committed to them today."

Gently, we then asked Brittany about Jesus' own claims to be God and the only way of salvation. "I think that was just his followers making claims about him that he didn't really make for himself," she said matter-of-factly. "I've read some of those passages in the Bible, and I am convinced that they were just later additions by his followers."

We could continue citing our conversation with Brittany or hundreds of other Millennials, but you get the point. There was great confusion over any of our questions about Jesus Christ because there were so many definitions of the person of Jesus. Here are some examples.

Jesus as the only way of salvation. While 31 percent strongly agreed with this statement, the diverse views of both Jesus and the means of salvation confused the issue. Some of the positive respondents interpreted the statement to indicate the need to follow the teachings of salvation; belief in Christ thus became a form of works salvation. Others (26 percent) did indicate that salvation was not works oriented, but some in that response saw Jesus as one of several choices as a giver of grace. Again, at the risk of redundancy, we see the number of true Christians in this generation to be somewhere around 15 percent.

2 .   **The person of Jesus.** The Millennial Generation was evenly divided on the sinlessness of Jesus. Exactly one-half of the respondents said that Jesus committed sins while he was on Earth; likewise one-half said that he did not commit sins. Most of the conversations we had with Millennials included positive comments about Jesus. There is just a lot of confusion and disagreement on who Jesus really is.

3.   **Belief in the afterlife or heaven.** Interestingly the Millennials want to believe that life does not end with cessation of our human mortality. Nearly 45 percent agreed strongly with the statement, "Heaven is a real place, not just a concept." Another 25 percent agreed somewhat with the same statement. Eric was one of those seven out of ten Millennials who agreed with the statement.

"Sure I believe in heaven," he began. "There seems to be plenty of evidence that life doesn't end when we die. I really don't give it much thought though. I guess when I do I find myself hoping there is life after death, and that there's a heaven. But overall I just think the evidence is strong for an afterlife."

We then asked him about his understanding of what the Bible says about heaven. "I really don't worry about that.

I'm not sure what's really true in the Bible and what's not true," Eric said. "I just think that more and more scientific evidence points to a life beyond this life. That's where I put my hope."

4. **Belief in hell and Satan.** Though the response was not as strong as their belief in heaven, 60 percent of Millennials believe hell is a literal place rather than a metaphorical concept. An identical 60 percent also believe that Satan (we also identified him as the devil) is a real being rather than just a symbol of evil.

5. **Beliefs about God.** The Millennials as a whole are a theistic group. They believe that God exists and that there is only one God. More than 72 percent agree that God is a real being and not just a concept. That same significant majority, 72 percent, assigns traditional theistic and Christian concepts to God. They believe he is all-powerful, all-knowing, and perfect in all he does. And they believe he is the Creator of the universe who rules the world today.

6. **Clarity among the confusion.** Okay, we know that all of these numbers and statistics can get boring or confusing or both. Just because the two of us are finance majors who enjoy numbers doesn't give us the right to put you to sleep. Allow us then to bring some level of clarity to the hodgepodge of statistics about the Millennials.

First, we can say that for most Millennials matters of religion are significantly less important than for previous generations. Nearly three-fourths of the generation call themselves spiritual but not religious. Those numbers tell us that most Millennials are theistic and are not antireligion or anti-Christian. But the numbers also tell us that matters of religion are not the focus for most of this generation.

Second, the ambivalence of most Millennials toward religion in general is evident in their beliefs about the Bible. Only one-fourth of the generation agrees strongly that the Bible is the written Word of God and is totally accurate in all that it teaches. Danielle from Colorado Springs reflects well this sentiment. "I think the Bible has a lot to offer," she informs us. "But I don't think that we can say that it is some kind of magical book that has all truth in it. I have read some parts of it before, but it's really not something I'm super interested in."

Third, the Millennial Generation is largely anti-institutional church in its attitude. An amazing 70 percent of these young adults agree that American churches are irrelevant today. This skepticism is not limited to non-Christians. Even Millennial Christians express doubts about the effectiveness of local churches around our nation. Throughout our interviews we heard comments like "tradition bound" and "irrelevant" and "focus on themselves" to describe American churches. These comments were pervasive and indicate that the challenge for churches to connect with the Millennials is significant and growing. We will explore this challenge more fully in the next chapter.

In summary we can say that the church's challenge is not overcoming an adversarial attitude from the Millennials. The true challenge is overcoming apathy. Christianity is not the belief of the vast majority of this generation. And they believe the American church to be one of the least relevant institutions in society.

The Parental Factor

As we have discussed at numerous points earlier in this book, the Millennials are strongly connected to their parents. We cited how important family is to this generation. Indeed there is not a close second in importance. Family was deemed really important in life by 61 percent of the Millennials. The second most important factor was friends, at only 25 percent.

Again, once we delve into all the family matters, the relationship between parents and Millennials is nothing less than remarkable. More than one-half (51 percent) of the generation says that their parents have a strongly positive influence on their lives. Another 37 percent say the influence is somewhat positive. The remainder of the Millennials say that parents have no influence (9 percent) or negative influence (3 percent).

Let's summarize these astounding statistics once more. Nearly nine out of ten (88 percent) of the Millennials look to their parents as a positive influence, and only 3 percent view the parents negatively. Also, recall from an earlier chapter that 85 percent of the Millennials look to their parents as their primary source of advice and guidance.

We are repeating these numbers for two reasons. First, we want to remind you of the powerful influence of parents on this generation. Second, we need to see how this influence affects Millennials in matters of faith and religion.

In the subjective portion of our study, we noticed an interesting and significant trend. Millennials tend to follow the examples of their parents in matters of faith, but they also tend to take the level of commitment one step further. For example, a Millennial with parents who were nominal Christians is likely to divorce himself or herself altogether from Christianity and churches. But a Millennial whose parents demonstrated some fervency in their Christian faith is likely to become even more fervent.

The bottom line is that most Millennials will not be lukewarm in their Christian faith. Most of them have made the decision not to embrace Christianity and to be forthright about their beliefs. Again, for them religion is not a major issue as it was with their parents. Many of their parents at least affirmed some low level of Christian commitment. The Millennial children no longer will play that game. The vast majority is declaring that religion in general, and Christianity in particular, is not high on their list of priorities.

Mark is in the oldest group of Millennials in our study. He was born in 1980. He describes his parents as "Easter/Christmas" Christians, meaning that they rarely attended church beyond those two Christian holidays. In the Bible Belt state of Alabama where he spent most of life, it was somewhat expected for Boomers to be affiliated with a church, even if the commitment to the church was virtually nonexistent.

"I have tried to understand why my parents are the way they are," Mark explained. "It's difficult for me to get why they thought it was necessary to have the pretense of being Christian when their actions said otherwise. I know there were certain cultural expectations, but it still makes little sense to me. Don't get me wrong. I love Mom and Dad very much. They've both been influential in my life. I just don't see any need for me to play the church game like they do. It's just not that important to me."

Mark declares himself to be theistic, a belief in one god. But he has not embraced the Christian faith, and he views religion in general to be relatively unimportant in his life.

There is, however, another perspective to the parental influence of the Christian faith on Millennials. In most cases where the parents showed true commitment to Christ and to their local church, their children have embraced that faith for themselves. But like Mark, who took his parents' nominal commitment one step further, a few Millennials will take a true commitment one step further to a fervent commitment. These Millennials will likely be few in number but may very well demonstrate the greatest Christian commitment of any generation in America's history.

These Millennials are the hope for the American church and for Christianity in America.

There Is Indeed Hope

You have to wonder what was going on in their minds. They had been on a roller coaster of emotions. Many of them followed him as he taught and performed miracles from town to town. And many saw him as the great hope and great promise.

But then came the cross, that awful tree of suffering and torture. Many of them saw him crucified. They saw his anguish. They saw his suffering. And they saw his death.

Three days after his death, word began to travel throughout the region. Some claimed that they saw him, that he was alive. Indeed the apostle Paul would later testify that he appeared to more than five hundred at one time (1 Cor. 15:6). There was no doubt. Death could not contain him. He was alive.

In the first chapter of Acts, we learn that Jesus spoke with them one last time. He commanded them not to leave Jerusalem until the promise of the Holy Spirit was fulfilled. Perhaps those words seemed curious. Why would they leave Jerusalem when he was right there with them? They certainly would have no desire to leave him.

And then it happened. As he concluded his last words to them, he was taken in a cloud. He was gone. They obviously were stunned because they continued to gaze in the sky even though he was no longer visible. Two angels, described by Luke in Acts 1:10 as "men in white clothes," told them to stop gazing at the sky and go wait.

Wait on what? We can't imagine all the thoughts that raced through their minds. Were they afraid? Were they discouraged? Were they confused?

After all these developments, they were simply told to wait.

And so they did. Peter, John, James, Andrew, Philip, Thomas, Bartholomew, Matthew, James the son of Alphaeus, Simon the Zealot, and Judas the son of James.

They were joined by unnamed women, except one. She was Mary, the mother of Jesus. The brothers of Jesus also joined them.

And they waited.

They waited in an upstairs room in Jerusalem. Not much other detail is provided except to say that most of their waiting was spent in prayer.

Ultimately Luke tells us, about 120 were gathered in this upper room. As Acts 2 unfolds, we read the vivid description of the day of Pentecost. There was a sound like a violent rushing wind. Flames of fire seemed to rest on each of them gathered. And they spoke in different languages so that the people who came for Pentecost could understand what was being said in each of their own languages.

So what became of that 120, that meager number of followers of Christ? Some would die for their beliefs. All were fervent about their faith. Stated simply and succinctly, that 120 turned the world upside down. History would forever change as the calendar flipped from BC to AD. They were the original carriers of the gospel message around the world.

Just a few followers of Christ. A few passionate followers of Christ. Indeed they turned the world upside down.

While we would not suggest the present-day Millennial Generation is preparing for another experience of Pentecost, we do see some parallels worth noting.

First, the Millennial Christians are relatively few in number. Again, we are reticent to estimate with any claim of precision, but we have suggested that the number of Christians in this generation is 15 percent of their total. In round numbers, let's just say there are twelve million Millennial Christians.

You're right. Twelve million is a lot more than 120. But in the context of 300 million U.S. residents or a world population of nearly seven billion, the number is small.

But what we learned about this relatively small number of Millennial Christians is that they are passionate about their faith. They have no patience for business as usual. They see the urgent need to share the gospel and to start new churches. And they will not wait on tired, established churches to get the work done.

"I'm not antichurch," Leslie explained to us. Leslie grew up in a Christian home. She appreciates her parents' clear convictions and sacrificial service in the church where they continue today. "But so much of what takes place in my parents' church is just keeping the doors open. Pay the staff. Keep the building nice. And give 10 percent or more of the church's income for someone else to do missions," she told us almost breathlessly.

"But that's plodding Christianity," she continued. "It has no urgency about it. It's more concerned about the people in the church than those outside the church. It breaks my heart that people are going to hell each day while so many churches have members who argue about Roberts Rules of Order or which members will serve on the personnel committee. We just don't have time for such foolishness."

Though some of their fervency may need some wise guidance, the Millennial Christians have a burning fire within them that can revolutionize churches to make a kingdom difference. How will churches in America respond? Will they embrace the energy and zeal of the Millennials, or will they disregard this generation and force these young people to venues of ministry beyond existing churches?

What will it take for churches today to embrace the Millennials and to capture their passion for reaching their neighborhoods and for reaching the nations? What will it take for churches to reach the rest of the nearly seventy-eight million Millennials who are not Christians? We know that the statistics on the American church are dismal and have been so for nearly half a century.

We see the presence of the Millennial Generation as a great opportunity offering much hope for the coming years. But the American church cannot do business as usual. Many changes are sorely needed.

There is indeed hope. To that topic we now turn in the next chapter.

CHAPTER 11

The Church Responds to the Millennials

Katie Davis grew up in Brentwood, Tennessee. Her home is just a few miles from where Thom lives today. Brentwood is a mostly affluent suburb of Nashville. Many of the country music stars and well-known Christian artists call Brentwood and the surrounding areas home. Katie had many of the economic advantages of the more affluent in her generation.

Katie is a Millennial, born in 1988. She is also part of the minority of Millennials who are Christians. She would clearly be one of the 15 percent who have unapologetically articulated Christian beliefs and lifestyles.

In December 2006, at the age of eighteen, Katie traveled to Uganda for the first time. She immediately began to love the Ugandan people and their culture. She met Pastor Isaac Wagaba, who asked her to come teach kindergarten at his orphanage in Buziika, called Canaan Children's Transit Center.

Katie returned to Uganda in the summer of 2007 to teach kindergarten at Canaan. As she walked the children home from class each day, she was surprised to see a number of school-aged children sitting idly on the side of the road or working in the fields. Few public schools exist in Uganda, and there were none in the area where Katie was working. Most schools are privately run and require fees for attendance. Because of the extreme poverty in Uganda, most children are simply unable to afford schooling.

Katie could not ignore the situation. She initiated a child sponsorship program, matching orphaned children who could not afford schooling with sponsors in the United States. The effort eventually became known as Amazima Ministries. For only three hundred dollars per year, sponsors send these children to school and provide school supplies, hot meals each day, and all necessary minor medical care. While Katie originally hoped to match forty children through the sponsorship program, 150 had enrolled by January 2008.

Today Uganda is the home of Katie Davis. The child sponsorship program continues to grow and care for more Ugandan children. Remarkably Katie has taken custody of fourteen children herself. When most people in their early twenties are just beginning their careers and families, Katie is the single parent of more than a dozen children who came to her with often severe and significant needs.

Is Katie Davis unique among Millennials? The answer is not a simple yes or no but requires a deeper understanding of the psyche of many of these young people.

On the one hand, the answer is a clear "yes." One would be hard pressed to find many in any generation who have made the type of commitment exemplified by Katie Davis. Indeed, not many of us have adopted fourteen children by our twenty-first birthday. In that regard she is definitely unique.

On the other hand, the mind-set of Katie Davis is pervasive among Millennial Christians. And though the Christian population of this generation is likely no higher than 15 percent, these young people may well turn the world upside down with their commitments and causes.

As we will share more fully later in this chapter, Millennial Christians are not content with business-as-usual churches. To the contrary, they will connect with churches only if those churches are willing to sell out for the sake of the gospel. The Millennial Christians abhor churches that focus inwardly, and they are more concerned about meeting their own needs than those of the community and the nations.

The Millennial Christians *will* commit themselves to churches. But those churches cannot look like and act like most American churches today. The Millennial church will be a radically committed church. More on that shortly.

Arden and the Other 85 Percent

Arden was born in 1989, four years after Jess was born. While Jess represents the minority Christian population of the Millennials, Arden is part of the larger segment, the other 85 percent who are not Christians.

In the previous chapter we looked at the strange religious world of this generation. In some ways it is difficult to be precise with religious descriptors for the Millennials. We know, however, that only 13 percent of the generation indicated that any kind of religion was really important in their lives. And we know that seven out of ten believe that the church is irrelevant, regardless of their religious beliefs.

So, in our interviews with Arden, we have to keep in mind that there really is no stereotypical Millennial regarding religious beliefs. But Arden does represent the majority because he is not a Christian.

In this book we have attempted to present and represent this generation as objectively as possible. We understand that total objectivity is not possible, but we have made every effort to reach this goal. In the previous chapter our Christian and Evangelical bias was more obvious since much of the discussion was viewed from an Evangelical perspective. In this chapter we explicitly bring our biases back because we are interested in how we Christians can be more effective in reaching the "Ardens" of this generation.

You see, not too many years ago, you would expect Arden to be a Christian because of his background. He was born and raised near Birmingham, Alabama, right in the heart of the mythical Bible Belt. His parents were middle-class suburban-ites, and he recalls seeing "a church on almost every block near my home."

But Arden is not a Christian. The Bible Belt has become a Bible string. With the Millennials we can no longer assume that demographics can give us significant clues about religious affiliation.

"I don't think I ever went to church with my parents," Arden told us. "I think my grandparents on my mom's side attended church occasionally, but I'm not really sure about that. Look, I know you are trying to understand the religious preferences of my generation, so I'm trying to shoot straight with you. But the bottom line is that I really don't think of religion or church that much. It's just not on my radar."

A Tale of Two Challenges

The American church confronts two significant challenges as the Millennials become the dominant generation in our nation. The first challenge is to connect with the Christians who comprise this generation, those whose attitude is like Katie Davis, totally sold out to the gospel.

Most Millennial Christians see local churches as business as usual, focused inwardly, more concerned about the needs of the members than the needs of the community and the nations. The bad news is that most American churches are not attractive to Millennials because of the inward focus of these congregations. The good news is that the churches that are successful in attracting Millennial Christians may have some of the most dedicated members in generations.

On the one hand, congregations today are challenged to connect with Millennial Christians. On the other hand, they are also confronted with the challenge of reaching the larger group of Millennials, some 85 percent who are not Christians.

It is likely, however, that the challenges are not mutually exclusive goals. Some of the actions churches can take to reach the Millennial Christians will likely prove helpful in reaching the non-Christian portion of this generation as well. Let's first look at how churches can connect with Millennial Christians.

Connecting with Millennial Christians

The secondary definition of *radical* in most dictionaries we consulted was "going to the extreme, especially regarding change from accepted or traditional norms." The most common definition is "going to the root or the origin," a meaning we don't hear espoused that often.

For Millennial Christians both definitions have merit. Compared to that which is taking place in most American churches, the Millennials are expecting the church to change from accepted or traditional norms. But these Millennials do not seek change for change sake. They have a keen desire to practice the Christianity of the Bible, to move the twenty-first century church to become more like the first-century church.

In many ways therefore, these young adults seek to move the church to its roots or origin.

The earliest snapshot of the Christian church can be found in Acts 2:42–47:

> And they devoted themselves to the apostles' teaching, to fellowship, to the breaking of bread, and to prayers.
>
> Then fear came over everyone, and wonders and signs were being performed through the apostles. Now all believers were together and had everything in common. So they sold their possessions and property and distributed the proceeds to all, as anyone had a need. Every day they devoted themselves to meeting together in the temple complex, and broke bread from house to house. They ate their food with a joyful and humble attitude praising God and having favor with all the people. And every day the Lord added to them those who were being saved.

The radical nature of Millennial Christianity thus includes the desire to forfeit material gain for the sake of others, a fierce devotion to Bible study ("the apostles' teaching"), an intense prayer life, and a total commitment to reach and minister to others in their communities and among the nations. What, then, must churches today do to attract these radical Christians?

Become radically committed to the community. For most Boomer churches, the community was perceived to be a place where prospects could be found. Entire systems of outreach were devised to find people to increase the membership of the church. In many of these churches, the community was seen to be a source of greater attendance and increased financial gifts.

Millennial Christians resist this view of the community. For them community is not a place where we look for prospects to help our church; it is a place where Christians are called to serve and minister. Millennials don't ask what the community can do for the church; they ask what they can do for the community.

Karen was twenty-four years old at the time of our interview with her. She grew up in a more established Southern Baptist church in South Carolina. Though she still resides in her home state, she now attends a church with no denominational affiliation. "I love the town where I live. But I've learned to love this community from my church. The pastor and other leaders in the church are constantly letting us know how we can have an impact where we live. Our church has been so consistent with caring for and loving our community that leaders from town now turn to us when they have a need. We don't have to have an outreach program," she said, remembering her former church, "because we are already in the community and because the community comes to us."

Two of the buzzwords used by Christian Millennials are *missional* and *incarnational*. *Missional* means that Christians are sent in the community, that they are on mission in the community. The community is not just a place where the church is located; it is a place where Christians are sent to demonstrate the love of Christ. Most Millennial Christians do not go to work, to the shopping center, or to the schools merely to carry out transactions. They see themselves as missionaries wherever they are in the community.

Millennials also are committed to being incarnational in the community as well. The word literally means "in the flesh" or physically present. But for this younger generation it has the deeper meaning of being present as a representative for Christ. As Karen told our research team, "When I am in my community, I try to see the people I encounter through the eyes of Christ. It makes all the difference in the world."

Millennial Christians will reject churches that tend to view the community as little more than a population pool from which growth in attendance and budget can come. But they will embrace churches that teach members to love the community.

You can tell the difference in these churches rather easily. In most churches, efforts to reach the community may be limited to distributing flyers telling residents about church events they can or should attend. "I don't criticize those churches," Karen told us. "But I want to be helping repair homes, caring for merchants who lost loved ones, and cleaning up trash for elderly residents. I know it's cliché, but I want to ask the question, 'What would Jesus do?' I want to be in the churches that view the community that way."

2. **Go deep in biblical teaching.** Millennial Christians are seeking to move as close to New Testament Christianity as possible. They have a deep hunger to learn more about Scripture. They understand that they are a relatively small minority in

their generation, and they want to be unwavering about their beliefs and convictions. Diluted doctrine and anemic biblical teaching and preaching are huge turnoffs for most Millennial Christians.

Cassandra was a relatively new Christian at the time of our interview with her. She was invited to a church worship service by a coworker. The twenty-eight-year-old Millennial had almost no church background in her immediate family. "I think I remember attending an Easter worship service when I stayed with my cousins," she recalled.

But Cassandra was taken aback by the services she attended with her coworker. "Yeah, I was blown away," she said emphatically. "The people there were so friendly, not friendly in a syrupy, fake kind of way but real and sincere. The music was great too. But it was the preaching that really blew me away. I learned more about the Bible in thirty minutes than I had my entire life. But I didn't feel like he was shoving stuff down my throat. He seemed to care about what he preached and those of us he preached to."

Thinking that the church she attended that Sunday was typical of other churches, Cassandra began visiting other congregations. She lived over twenty miles from the church where her coworker had invited her, and she really wanted something closer.

"Was I disappointed!" she said with no small measure of frustration. "I thought I could find a church just like my friend's church. It didn't take many visits to other churches to realize that few churches raise the bar for biblical teaching and preaching.

I'm just not going to a church that doesn't take the Bible seriously. That's why I'm traveling nearly fifty miles round trip to go to this church [the first church she visited]."

A defining characteristic of Millennial Christians is their serious approach to the Bible and their faith. They are not content with their parents' lukewarm faith.

Our study supported this reality in a number of ways. One of the clearest was how we asked Millennials if they were Christians. When we asked in general terms if they were Christian, nearly two-thirds affirmed the label. But when we began to ask with more detailed questions of belief, the response grew smaller. For example, 20 percent of this generation could affirm that they were born-again Christians as we asked questions that came closer to the basics of the Christian faith. But only 6 percent could affirm statements that we categorized as "Evangelical." That number was so small that we are unable to use the data from this group because the sample size is not adequate.

Our point is that the more we defined Christianity in terms of its biblical and historical roots, the smaller the response. But we noticed something else that was rather interesting. The smaller response groups were more vociferous about and committed to their faith. For example, 82 percent of born-again Christians said they considered their faith important to their lives.

Cassandra, in our preceding story, is representative of the committed Christians in our study. She wants to know biblical truths. She wants to learn from biblical teachers who teach the Bible in a way that she can constantly be challenged and consistently learn more about Scripture. She wants to hear sermons from preachers who delve into the riches of the texts of Scripture. She sees no dichotomy between relevance and biblical depth.

Some churches in America will likely continue to decline and weaken because their leaders and members refuse to get out of their comfort zones. These churches will continue to have mediocre Bible study groups and anemic preaching. Not only will these churches fail to attract the non-Christian Millennials; they will forfeit the opportunity to reach Millennial Christians. Christians who are members of America's largest generation will not embrace churches where the Bible is not taught and preached with depth and convictions.

(3) **Love the nations.** Frank and Karen are good friends of ours. They are close to Jess' age, and their parents are Thom's peers. We are not telling you their real names or the country where they are currently located because we fear for their safety.

Frank and Karen are living in a predominantly Muslim country. They provide Bible studies for local residents, and they share the gospel whenever they can. They are passionate about caring for the nations of the world and taking to them the gospel of Jesus Christ.

Not too long ago they received a note that contained a threat to kill them if they did not refrain from their Christian activities. They were not certain if the name on the note was the real identity of the one who threatened them. But the name on the note was that of a prominent Muslim leader.

At risk were their lives and the lives of their young children. What was their response? Though they are exercising more caution in their activities, they haven't stopped their Bible studies and their witnessing. They are willing to sacrifice their lives for the sake of their beliefs.

Frank and Karen's attitude is not atypical of Millennial Christians. The Bible says to love the nations, and so they do. The Bible says to take the gospel throughout the world, and so they do. The Bible says to forsake all for the cause of Christ, and so they do.

Some would say they are practicing radical Christianity. Though they would likely agree, they see this radical Christianity as normative Christianity in the Bible.

Churches that attract Millennial Christians must demonstrate unwavering love for the nations. Just how then is this love demonstrated? Listen to the perspective of Jason, twenty-one years old at the time of our interview.

"I guess I am one of a small number in my generation that grew up going to church," he began. "I love my parents, and I appreciate the fact that they showed so much love for our church. But I'm just not where they are about the local church and missions."

We asked him to clarify that last statement.

"Well," he said with obvious discomfort, "for my parents, missions means giving to the church, which will then send funds for others to do mission work. They believe they have been obedient when they give their money for someone else to do the work."

Jason continued, "Don't get me wrong. I want churches to give a lot of their funds for mission work. It's not that part that I question. It's just that when all we do is give our money, it's not enough. We need to be involved in missions around the world. We need to be getting our hands and feet dirty. We need to be personally involved as well as giving."

Then Jason said something we heard from many Millennial Christians. "If you take the Bible seriously, you've got to love people. But you've got to demonstrate that love. That's why we are serious about missions. And that's why we are serious about adoption. Most Christians want to ignore James 1:27. But my generation takes that verse literally."

The verse he mentioned is as follows: "Pure and undefiled religion before our God and Father is this: to look after orphans and widows in their distress and to keep oneself unstained by the world."

This is the generation of Christians that will take the mandate of missions by storm. This is the generation that will adopt the orphans around the world. And this generation will not be satisfied with missions that are limited to paying for others to do the work. That is just the beginning.

Business-as-usual churches doing missions by proxy will not see an influx of Millennials. Such churches will miss a major opportunity to see a transformation of their congregations by God.

Direct revenue outwardly. Millennial Christians are not reticent to speak up about church finances. They often lament how many dollars of the church budget are directed toward looking after the needs of the existing membership and how few dollars go to the mission fields of the community, the nation, and the world.

"I call it Baby Boomer reflux," said Rebecca. The outspoken twenty-six year old clarified: "The Boomers give money to the church, but it comes right back to them to keep them content. They hire the staff to do the ministry they won't do. The money goes to make the buildings more comfortable for them. And then churches begin all kinds of ministries for boomers and their families to keep them happy. Most churches today suffer from Baby Boomer reflux."

We didn't have to ask Rebecca if she would attend that kind of church. "I'll never go to that kind of church," she responded without a question. "That's not New Testament Christianity. That's a religious social club."

Millennial Christians are scrutinizing carefully how churches are spending the money of the tithes and offerings given by the members. They are looking to see if the church truly is a Great Commission church or a church seeking great comfort. They are asking questions about the dollars given to missions. Where does the money really go? What happens to the money after it arrives at its destination? How efficient are the recipients of the funds in getting the money directly to mission needs? How much of the mission dollars go to administration and overhead?

Baby Boomer and Gen X Christians were more likely to accept the traditional ways churches give to missions without many questions. Not so with the Millennial Christians. Because they are such a small minority in their generation, they know how precious the resources are to reach the community and beyond. They will thus examine the stewardship of funds in a church or denomination with great scrutiny. They will ask many questions. And they will be unwilling to stay in churches they perceive to be irresponsible with the money entrusted to them.

But the good news is that Millennial Christians will be attracted to those congregations that show wise stewardship of their funds. They will be excited about churches that sacrificially give for the cause of missions in their communities and throughout the world.

5. **Demonstrate transparency, humility, and integrity.** In our interviews with Millennial Christians, we heard those three words frequently. They typically mentioned them in reference to church leaders. Transparent leaders are, to use the words of one Millennial, "sincere men and women who don't have to wear a religious mask. We know that these leaders have the same challenges and struggles we do."

On more than one occasion a Millennial Christian told us they are particularly troubled about how some church leaders "speak a strange religious language when they are talking to other Christians." Noted another Millennial, "I just want them to be real. There seems to be a lot of false piety with some leaders."

Though we did not do a word count, we would not be surprised if "humility" was the number one virtue of church leaders that Millennials desired. This desire is not the result of haughty televangelists or pushy preachers they have known. It is simply the Millennials' understanding of Scripture that calls for humility among all Christians, particularly among Christian leaders.

These young adult Christians seem to have a keen radar that picks up easily on those who have a false humility. "I can smell false humility a mile away," noted Kevin, a twenty-year-old Christian. "It's worse to me than an arrogant leader. I just can't stand it."

By this point it should be no surprise that Millennial Christians are looking for churches where the leaders are people of unquestionable integrity. Again, they are not reacting to any negative situation as much as they are seeing how Scripture paints a portrait of a Christian leader.

Further, these young adult Christians are concerned about the testimony of character of the leaders of the churches and how that testimony may positively or negatively impact the witness of Christians and churches. Back to a point we made earlier in the chapter: Millennial Christians are passionate about incarnational missions and ministry in their communities and to the nations. Anything that hurts that effort, such as issues of leadership character, is seen as repulsive. Anything that moves that effort positively is readily embraced.

These are some of the key issues to connect with Christian Millennials. Keep in mind, however, that we estimate that only 15 percent of the generation is Christian. The even greater challenge is to reach the other 85 percent who are not likely Christian.

Reaching Non-Christian Millennials

Depending upon one's perspective as a Christian, these are either the best of times or the worst of times. One could, with good reason, lament the reality of the large number of unreached Millennials. One could also look at this generation as a great mission opportunity for churches throughout the nation. If the latter, more hopeful, view is embraced, there are some key issues to consider in reaching this generation.

Remember the indifference factor. In my (Thom's) experience as a church consultant working with hundreds of churches across our nation, I have noticed two perspectives on unchurched and unreached people as I speak with church leaders and members. The first perspective assumes that those who are not in church really want to be. The unchurched are more uninformed than they are antagonistic. The key to reaching them from this viewpoint is to get the information about the church to the community. Once they know about the church and all it offers, they will come.

The second perspective is the negative viewpoint of the unchurched. Those who are not Christians are antagonistic to matters of the faith. They will refuse to talk with us or listen to us. They like arguments. And they are likely to ridicule Christians they encounter.

In our studies of the unchurched over nearly a quarter of a century, we rarely see these non-Christians respond to Christians with eagerness or with antagonism. The response is typically somewhere in between the two extremes. In one recent study on the unchurched, we found that only 5 percent had an antagonistic attitude toward Christians, and only 11 percent of the unchurched were highly receptive to them.

But we are noticing a significant attitudinal shift with the 85 percent non-Christian Millennials. Their attitude toward Christians and churches is largely one of indifference.

Remember an earlier statistic we reported on this generation. Only 13 percent of the Millennials rated any kind of religious or spiritual issue as important. We are dealing with a new reality in reaching unchurched America with this generation. Most church outreach efforts used today will not be effective with this group. The challenge we have is that Christianity is not even on their radar. We have to be wise and discerning in reaching these young men and women. Allow us to make a few suggestions based on our research.

Unleash the simple power of inviting. Millennials as a whole are social creatures. Their desire to be with others is not limited to electronic social media. They value being physically present with family and friends. Unlike previous unchurched generations, they don't view the church with suspicion and doubt. For better or worse, they don't really think much about churches at all.

We noted in earlier research that unchurched Americans respond well to an invitation to church, especially if the one inviting takes them to church. We think this simple approach to reaching this generation will be even more powerful. Remember our story earlier in this chapter about Cassandra? She did not hesitate to join her coworker at church. And once she experienced the worship service, she was ready to find a church home. That simple invitation ultimately led her to becoming a Christian.

Millennial Christians need the encouragement and reminder to invite their friends to church. We doubt these young Christians will need much persuasion. They are mostly radical in their faith. If they learn that they can do something to advance the cause of the kingdom, they will likely do it.

3. **Connect Boomer parents with Millennial children.** These numbers are staggering. When asked if parents were a regular and key source of advice and guidance, 86 percent of the Millennials responded positively. In a similar question, 88 percent of the generation said that parental influence was positive.

Don't ignore these statistics as just another interesting set of numbers. Perhaps more than any generation in America's history, Millennials have incredibly strong relationships with their parents. We estimate there are about thirty million Boomers in churches today. Many of them have adult children who are not Christians. Though the approaches may vary, why can't churches become more intentional about connecting these Boomer Christians to their adult children who are not Christians?

The Millennials have already told us that they heed their parents' advice. And nine out of ten indicated that they considered their parents' guidance positively. Churches need to be about the task of reminding and equipping Boomers who attend that they must be sources of positive guidance to move their adult children closer to the faith.

4. **Demonstrate the deep meaning of following Christ.**
Nearly nine out of ten Millennials believe it is their responsibility to change the world. An incredibly high 96 percent of the generation believes they can do something great. But almost nine out of ten feel that they have a lot of unused potential.

Admittedly some of these attitudes reflect the idealism of youth. But we are seeing more than passing idealism in this generation. Recall our earlier discussion of the incredible impact of September 11, 2001, on this generation, an event we believe affected the Millennials as much as the assassinations of John Kennedy, Martin Luther King Jr., and Bobby Kennedy did the Baby Boomers.

The Millennials view life through the lens of the threats of terrorism. Life is tenuous and uncertain. Changes must be made quickly. Trivial matters should be ignored to focus on more weighty matters.

We believe this is one major reason this generation wants to be a part of groups and organizations that make a difference. Unfortunately one of the reasons they are indifferent toward American churches is that they don't see these churches as having a significant impact on the world. That is the bad news.

The good news is, the unchurched Millennials will likely be attracted to churches that demonstrate in deep biblical teaching and preaching what it really means to be followers of Christ. These young men and women truly want to be part of something that is bigger than themselves.

At the risk of redundancy, we remind you that Millennials, both Christians and non-Christians, are not impressed with most American churches today. They see them as religious social clubs that focus on themselves rather than the needs of others. But if this generation is ever convinced that churches are serious about a radical commitment to Christ, we have good reason to be hopeful to connect with both the Christians and the non-Christians of this generation.

5. **Demonstrate concern for others.** I wish we had comparable questions of previous generations, but the Millennials may prove to be the most activist generation we have known for over a century. Nearly eight out of ten already have a strong motivation to serve others in society. And unlike the Baby Boomers, who were activists in their own ways, the Millennials are motivated more by helping others than seeking their own preferences.

That is why if you see a church with a large number of Millennials, you are likely to see a church that is passionate about serving its community and passionate about reaching the nations with the gospel. You are also likely to see a church that commits a significant portion of its budget to caring for the needs of others and reaching out to others with the gospel. Simply stated, Millennial churches are others-focused rather than self-focused.

Ironically, it may be the largely self-centered Baby Boomers who instilled this desire for serving others in their children. Boomers, perhaps in reaction to a weaker connection with their own parents, made valiant efforts to have healthy and open relationships with their children. We heard in countless interviews how the Millennials connect well with and look up to their parents.

Though their moms and dads could and still can be "helicopter" parents hovering over their children, the Millennials grew up with the example of a mom and dad who served them and gave sacrificially for them. It seems as if that attitude of servant-hood has transferred to another generation. But Millennials' desire to serve others extends beyond family. They want to serve the community. They want to serve the world. They want to make a difference. And many will be willing to go to those churches that demonstrate such traits.

6. Demonstrate transparency, humility, and integrity . . . again. Like their Christian peers, the Millennials who are not Christians have little patience for leaders who don't demonstrate integrity and who demonstrate self-centeredness and arrogance. Luke is not a Christian, but the twenty-five-year-old from Missouri has a perspective that is common with his generation. "I just can't stand leaders who are full of themselves," he said with the typical forthrightness of his generation. "I see it in politicians. I see it in the business world. I see it in Hollywood. And I see it in religious leaders. They totally lack integrity. You never know when they are lying."

We believe Luke would have been willing to modify his statements not to be all-inclusive if we had pressed them. There are some good leaders in politics, business, Hollywood, and churches. But his point is well taken. Millennials have a keen sensitivity to these issues. They are looking for leaders who represent the best of biblical values, whether they know they originate from the Bible or not.

The Hinge Generation?

We see Millennials as the hinge generation for the American church. They are largely non-Christian, 85 percent by our estimates. By hinge we mean that the door of opportunity could shut or open widely. If American churches only reach the 15 percent of Christians in the generation, we will see massive numbers of church closings and even more church declines. If the churches reach less than the 15 percent, the terrible scenario will even be worse.

But the door could swing the other way. Churches could make the radical changes necessary to connect with both the Christian and non-Christian parts of this generation. If such significant change takes place, churches in America could see their best days ever.

The current evidence supports the more distressing scenario. Current trends in most American churches are anything but healthy. From a human perspective the situation looks bleak.

But as Christians we don't always view outcomes based on the perspectives of humans. We know the evidence of how God sometimes surprises the world with His unexpected and incredible intervention. In many ways His coming as a man named Jesus to intervene and offer salvation to the world was a surprise to many. We remain confident that the God who cannot be contained in a box of human reason may still have a great work to do in the churches in America.

It is our prayer that we will respond with obedience.

Radical obedience.

Our Thanks

Thank you for allowing us to look at the Millennial Generation through the lens of our faith. We have tried to remain objective throughout the book, but we did want to speak to the churches and church leaders who need to connect with this generation before it's too late.

Our journey in this research about the Millennial Generation is almost done. Join us in the final brief chapter as we offer a few summary thoughts.

Here Come the Millennials!

They are the largest generation in America's history, some seventy-eight million born between 1980 and 2000. Their influence and impact are already being felt in businesses, schools, churches, and political institutions. And that influence will only grow stronger. Like the other large American generation, the Baby Boomers, this generation will get a lot of attention. This book is but one example.

Schools are already wondering how to connect with them.

Businesses are already trying to market to them.

Politicians are already trying to get their votes.

Churches are already trying to reach them and keep them.

The sheer size of the Millennials, of course, is sufficient reason to know as much about this generation as possible. But there are other reasons, many more reasons in fact. We have attempted to share some of those reasons in this book, and we hope we made some contribution to the growing body of knowledge about this generation.

It seems that many of the pundits about this generation have a clear opinion regarding the positive or negative contributions the Millennials may ultimately make. Some see them as spoiled and self-serving; others see them as the panacea for most of our nation's ills.

Of course the reality is neither extreme. Like any generation, Millennials have both good and bad attributes. And like any generation, there are wide varieties of characteristics and personalities among the millions represented. Count us, however, among those who are positive about the Millennials. While we don't have a blind eye to the challenges they may present, we believe they have much to offer now and even more to offer in the years to come. This is a generation that desires to serve, that is willing to listen, that seeks counsel and advice, that loves family, and that truly desires to make a difference.

Tom Brokaw coined the phrase "the Greatest Generation" to describe those who lived through the Great Depression, fought in World War II, and contributed to the great productivity of America during the war and after the war. The children of the Greatest Generation are the Baby Boomers, that largely self-centered and indulgent generation.

But the grandchildren of the Greatest Generation are the Millennials, and we will go out on a metaphorical limb and project that these young adults will eventually become "the

Greatest Generation, part 2." Many of the qualities and characteristics of the Greatest Generation seem to have skipped to
their grandchildren.

Allow us, then, to offer these summary comments that
highlight this new and potentially great generation. We will be
watching them closely for years to come.

Family Focused

The Baby Boomers tend to be all about, well, Baby Boomers.
Millennials are more about serving others than self. That reality
was made clear in our research about their attitudes regarding
family. Perhaps it is premature to project that the Millennials
will lower the divorce rate, reduce spouse abuse significantly,
raise emotionally healthy children, and, as a consequence, lower
the crime rate. But we won't be surprised if all of those positive
trends are realized.

We were blown away by the attitudes of the Millennials
about the family. They seemed to have a maturity well beyond
their years. And they seem to understand clearly the mistakes
of previous generations. They are determined not to repeat
them.

Anyone seeking to understand and connect with this generation must grasp their love and commitment to their families.
They will choose vocations that allow them to spend more time
with their families. They will spend money on goods and services they perceive benefit their families. They will be loyal to
institutions that help them strengthen their families.

Our second choice for a title for this book was *The Family Generation*. You truly can't understand the Millennials until you understand their commitment to their families.

Looking for Guidance

Most Millennials don't pretend to have all the answers. They have a humility about them that is unusual for their relative youthfulness. Many of them have looked to their parents for advice and guidance all of their lives. They are still connected to their parents, but they don't want to limit their spheres of influencers just to Mom and Dad.

They are looking for true mentors in the workplace. They don't want merely disseminators of knowledge in educational institutions; they want men and women who are examples through their lives as well as their words. They will avoid institutions that treat them like one of the masses; but they will flock to institutions that have transparent and servantlike leaders.

This is the generation that may teach us how to respect people again. They are already showing respect to one another. They already have a deep respect for those older than they are, something they undoubtedly learned in their relationship with their parents.

Those who are older than the Millennials have a great opportunity to influence this huge generation. They are not only willing to listen to you; they want to listen to you. But they want you to take time to guide them and to listen to them as well. They are eager to learn from you. But this opportunity to be a mentor, to be a leader, is not an indefinite opportunity. Leaders in families, governments, schools, churches, and other institutions can ill afford to wait.

A New Kind of Communication

Those who suppose that the Millennials are mostly the new purveyors of technology miss the point with this generation. Rapid technological advances have taken place all the Millennials' lives. They know no other world.

But what has happened uniquely with the Millennials is how they perceive communication. For one, communication is instantaneous and available 24-7. This generation is impatient when they have to wait on communication. The old print media experiences this reality every day. The Baby Boomer generation woke up each morning and read the daily newspaper.

Not so the Millennials. The news of the morning paper is old. It happened yesterday. They already know the events from the previous day. It's time to move forward.

Communication for the Millennials also knows few boundaries. Certainly few of this generation worry about barriers of geography and time. They connect to anyplace. They connect at anytime.

This is the generation that has learned the power of communication to effect change. Previous generations could certainly use forms of media to effect change as well, but it was rarely in real time. Woe is the organization that ignores the collective power of communication of this generation. It only takes a few minutes for Millennials to speak their minds on issues and organizations via Facebook, texting, blogs, and Twitter.

Millennials have both shaped and been shaped by a new kind of communication that no previous generation has known. The individuals and organizations that fail to understand this reality will fail to connect with America's largest generation.

A New Kind of Insecurity

We have yet to know fully the psychological and emotional impact of September 11, 2001, on the Millennials. We do have reason to believe that the infamous day in America's history may define this generation as much as any single event has ever defined a generation. We see at least two major reasons this may be the case.

First, 9-11 redefined the meaning of war for Americans. Prior to this point, war was something that took place in another country. Changing television channels or not reading the news could hide the horrors and tragedies of war for most families. Not so with the new war on terrorism.

The events of 9-11 meant that war is being waged on our own soil. It meant that the enemy could no longer be clearly defined as people of another country. It meant that the rules of war had changed. The enemy has no hesitancy to take innocent and defenseless lives. The new war is unpredictable. We are ever on alert. Airplanes are no longer just means of transportation; they are also weapons of war.

The Millennials have and are growing up with this new reality. The only sure things they know about the enemy are that he is ruthless, unpredictable, and has no rules of engagement. The war on terrorism is a constant war on their nerves and psyche.

Second, what took place on September 11, 2001, taught the Millennials that life is brief. Unlike many young people before them, they have an acute awareness that life is fragile and can end at any time. That likely explains why they are impatient and unwilling to accept business as usual. They can't wait forever for things to change because they know they don't have forever to wait.

A Distrust of Two Major Institutions

One of the few things Millennials have in common with their Baby Boomer parents is their distrust of the institutions of government and church. But unlike the Boomers, the Millennials' distrust is not due to lack of respect. To the contrary, we have shown that this generation has a high and unusual level of respect for most people.

For the Millennials, though, governments and churches have well earned their distrust. They see politicians who seem to have no moral constraints. They see elected officials who fail to make the tough decisions to put the country on a better path. They cringe at the destructive and argumentative nature of politics and government. They have lost respect for politics and politicians, and they are ready to make changes.

The institutional church is a mixed bag for Millennials. They still are spiritual, albeit in a nebulous sense. And they really would like to have a greater level of respect for organized religion.

But they witnessed the seemingly never-ending moral failure of pastors and priests. They perceive most churches, rightly so, as inwardly focused, not serving either the world or their communities. And, probably more than any other factor, they perceive the churches and their leaders to be negative and argumentative. The research indicates they have all but given up on local churches.

The two historically stalwart institutions of our nation, government and church, are in deep trouble with the Millennials. If current trends continue, the former will be changed radically, and the latter will be abandoned quickly.

The Great Reconcilers

Millennials as a whole are not weak in character or unwilling to deal with tough issues. But they are weary of the constant fighting, shouting, and negativity that shape many of our institutions and much of our media. This generation will be prone to be a reconciling generation. There will be many peacemakers among them.

As we indicated in this book, the members of America's largest generation simply can't understand why so many adults and groups can't get along. Those who will connect best with

Millennials in the years ahead will understand these heartfelt desires to be the great reconcilers.

The Impatient Generation

Perhaps it's because of September 11. Or maybe it's related to their parents' encouraging them to do whatever they wanted to accomplish. It could even be related to their ability to have instantaneous information and communications anywhere in the world.

This generation is in a hurry. They really don't think they have time to wait. They want to make a difference, but they want to make a difference now. They are confident in their own abilities but in a humble kind of way. They will gladly listen to advice and counsel within reason.

But don't tell them to wait. They just don't understand such logic. For them life is brief, and there is a whole world to change. They are not waiting any longer.

Here Come the Millennials

It's really an invasion that has taken most of us by surprise. The birth of seventy-eight million babies is huge, but it did take place over two decades. It has been sufficiently incremental that many of us did not notice the impact.

But now they are here. About half of them have already entered the workforce, and the other half is not far behind. And they are bringing changes wherever they are found. Their influence will grow and become more pervasive.

We believe that, for the most part, this generation will become one of the greatest generations our nation has known. We believe that our research and questions and conversations with the older part of this generation clearly point in that direction.

For certain we are convinced that this generation will make its mark. The question for us, then, is not one of the Millennials' impact on our nation and world. Our question is more one for those who are not Millennials. How will we receive them? How will we channel their ambitions and impatience? How will we work with them in greater service and healthy reconciliation? What will we do when they insist that institutions change and change immediately?

Are we ready for the Millennials?

We better be ready.

They are already here.

Here come the Millennials!

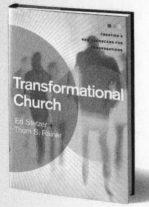

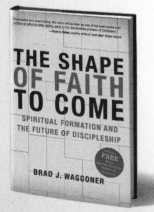
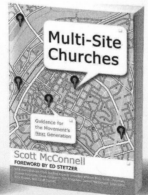